The Ultraliving Lessons

The Ultraliving Lessons

An Inspirational Guide
to the
Ultrarunning Way of Life

By Jordan Wickett

Copyright © Jordan Wickett, 2022

All rights reserved. Without limiting the rights under copyright reserved above, no part of this publication can be reproduced, stored in or introduced into a retrieval system, or transmitted, in any form, or by any means (electronic, mechanical, photocopying, recording, or otherwise) without the prior written permission of the copyright owner.

Disclaimer:
I have tried to recreate events, locales, and conversations from my memories of them. In order to maintain anonymity and protect privacy in some instances, I have changed the names of some individuals and places, or omitted or replaced personal names with a pseudonym. I also may have changed some identifying characteristics and details, such as physical properties, occupations, and places of residence.

The conversations in the book all come from my recollections, though they are not written to represent word-for-word transcripts. Rather, I have retold them in a way that evokes the feeling and meaning of what was said and in all instances, the essence of the dialogue is accurate.

The information in this book is meant to supplement, not replace, proper ultrarunning training. Like any sport involving speed, equipment, balance, and environmental factors, ultrarunning poses some inherent risk. I advise readers to take full responsibility for their safety and know their limits. Before practicing skills described in this book, be sure that any equipment is well maintained and do not take risks beyond your level of experience, aptitude, and comfort level.

ISBN: 979-8-8292828-6-8

Cover Design: Ellyl Faith Llavore
Cover Photo: Chris Henderson
Bruce Trail Map Designer: Peter Karas and Corinne Garlick

To my wife, Lindsay, and our children, Norah, James, and David.

Contents

Introduction 1

My Story 3
What is Ultrarunning? 7
What is Ultraliving? 8
My Qualifications 8
Why I Wrote This Book 8

Part One: The Ultraliving Lessons 11

Tour du Mont Blanc - August 2008 13
The Toronto Waterfront Marathon - October 2014 18
La Sauvage - August 2015 27
50 Miles on the Bruce Trail - November 2015 34
Sulphur Springs 50 km (Part 1) - May 2016 40
Haliburton Forest 50 Miler - September 2017 46
Sulphur Springs 100 Miler - May 2018 52
Squamish Running Weekend - June 2018 61
Horror Trail Race - October 2018 68
Sulphur Springs 50 km (Part 2) - May 2019 73
Quebec Mega Trail 110 km - June 2019 78
Midnight Moose 100 Miler - September 2019 86
FKT 99
Bruce Trail FKT Attempt (Part 1) – August 2021 111
Bruce Trail FKT Attempt (Part 2) - September 2021 123
Afterward 136

Part Two: The Ultraliving Manual 143

The Ultraliving Manual 145
Running Gear 147
    Shoes 147
    Hydration Packs 150
    Clothes 151
    Watches 154
    Additional Equipment 155

Audio	156
Ultramarathon Training	157
Logistics	157
Types of Training	161
Ultrarunning Training Plans	165
50 km Training Plan	167
50-Mile/100 km Training Plan	170
100-Mile Training Plan	173
Ultramarathon Racing	176
Race Day Preparation	176
Race Nutrition	178
Self-Care	181
Nutrition and Health	184
Three Big Lessons for Healthy Eating	184
Tactics for Healthy Eating	186
Managing Stress	189
Inspiration	192
Ultrarunning Influencers	192
Final Thoughts	203
References	205
Acknowledgements	210

Introduction

My Story

"Wickett, look at that big belly!" yelled Adam.

    The playful insult hit me like a ton of bricks. It was my grade 10 year of high school and I was on my way to football practice. I had been walking with some of the best-looking girls in school, a few ladies who played on the soccer team, and we were all headed to the sports fields just a short walk from the school. I knew that Adam didn't mean any harm. Two years older than me, Adam was a top track athlete and football player from another high school who was visiting for some special coaching. I was mortified by Adam's greeting, but I couldn't disagree with him. In football terminology, I had a big front porch, which meant that my belly hung out over my pants and well below my football jersey.

    High school had not been an easy time for me—I weighed 280 pounds, which was huge even on my six-foot-one frame. People in our small community of Chatham, Ontario, Canada seemed to have a hard time understanding why I was so overweight. My grandfather, Jack Parry, lived in Chatham for most of his life and was an Olympic athlete and Grey Cup–winning running back. My parents also grew up in Chatham and they were both accomplished athletes in high school. I definitely didn't fit the mould of my family.

A number of things led me to a moment of reckoning at that point in my life. Like any teenager in high school, I had developed a crush or two and had started paying special attention to the girls that I liked, though I wasn't getting any attention in return. I had certainly let my appearance slip, and I had a hard time finding clothes that fit me. I was appalled that I had become so out of shape. In gym class, I was winded from running for only a few minutes. When I was walking around town with my friends, I had a hard time keeping up and often asked my friends to slow down. Feelings of frustration and disappointment finally compelled me into action on a fateful night in the fall of 1996, my grade 10 year. Without putting much thought into it, I laced up my old athletic shoes and left for a nighttime run. I only ran for a short distance, keeping my run to around 15 minutes and mixing in walking. The running was difficult and I struggled my way through; however, I loved the feeling of moving outside and enjoyed the sense of accomplishment when I finished my run.

That was the first time I ran on my own and I knew that I was on to something. Gaining confidence from my run, I decided to try a weight workout at my local gym a week later. I fumbled my way around the gym and completed a short weight training session. Just like my run the week before, I relished the sense of accomplishment from my workout. I started going to the gym off and on for the next few weeks. After a month or two, I developed some consistency and started going to the gym at least three times per week. I would run on the treadmill or use the Stairmaster for 20 minutes and then lift weights for 40 minutes.

As the school year ended, I had become much stronger, but I didn't see any significant change to my appearance. I expressed my frustration to my dad one night while we were chatting before bed. My dad hesitated and then asked me if I had changed my diet. He was being careful not to hurt my feelings, but he knew that I needed this feedback. My dad's question stung a little bit. I wasn't proud of my eating habits, since I ate a lot of junk, including fast food, soda, and candy. After ruminating on this conversation for a while, I resolved that I was going to change my diet and, fortunately, I knew who to look to for guidance.

With blond hair, a kind smile, and an infectious laugh, my older sister Jacquie is beautiful. She's been in great shape her whole life and it was no different when I was in high school. Jacquie moved to Waterloo, Ontario in her grade 9 year to attend a special high school for athletes. She trained at figure skating for half the day and went to school for the other half. Jacquie came back to our family home on weekends and I took note of how she ate nutritious foods and controlled her portions.

Halfway through grade 11, I adopted the low-fat diet that Jacquie was following. Eating low-fat isn't ideal for athletes, but this diet was very popular at the time, and the combination of structured eating and exercise worked like a charm for me. I started dropping weight quickly and I was stunned to see 30 pounds melt away in two months.

Very pleased with my results, I doubled down on my efforts, paying extra attention to my diet and never missing a workout. I became a regular at the gym, lifting weights most days of the week and finishing my training sessions with a run. I lost another 40 pounds over the next four months and completely transformed my physique. As a result of all my efforts, I started my final year of high school in the best shape of my life. I weighed a solid 230 pounds and could bench press over 300 pounds.

I had a great senior year with high school football; I was named captain of the team and we made it to our regional semifinals. I also earned all-star and MVP of our team and received the award for the top male academic athlete in high school.

As high school ended, I was recruited to play football at the University of Waterloo and trained hard throughout the summer in preparation. I was so excited to be at the week-long training camp and expected the best. I didn't realize that I was about to start one of the most challenging periods of my life.

I pulled my hamstring early in training camp while being timed for the 40-yard dash. The pulled hamstring was a big blow to my performance during the rest of camp and the coaches put me on the practice squad as a result. I quickly learned that the practice squad often got beat up by the starting squad, and disaster struck during the end of the second week of training camp. I was playing linebacker in a drill against the starting offensive line, which had me hitting head-on-head during every repetition. There were three other linebackers in the drill with me, but they did the smart thing and sat out after a few reps. I was keen on proving myself and kept going. I took a blow to the head, waited 30 seconds, and then took another one. I realized that I wasn't feeling right after one particularly hard shot to the head. After a conversation with the trainer, it was evident that I had a significant concussion and I was told that I couldn't practice until I could do a stress test without any concussion symptoms. I didn't know much about concussion symptoms at that point, but I would soon find out.

I woke up the next day with the brain fog that I would come to know intimately. Brain fog is a general term that is the best way to describe the grogginess, heavy eyes, and mild depression that comes with post-concussion syndrome (PCS). I struggled my way through the first few weeks of university and was discouraged when the PCS symptoms did not go away. Routine tasks became exhausting and I often had to go back to my dorm room for a nap during the day while my classmates were studying and socializing. In high school, I coped with stressful situations by lifting weights; however, I found that strength training worsened my PCS symptoms. I stopped exercising altogether in an effort to speed up my recovery.

When I called my parents for some advice a few weeks into my first semester, I was in a bad spot. My dad recommended that I go running. He's a lawyer and used to run to help deal with the stress of law school, sometimes running twice per day during final exams. I took his advice and was so excited when I found that I could run at a slower pace without worsening my PCS symptoms. I started to run regularly and was extremely relieved to have exercise back in my life as a coping strategy. Though it would be a long time before I could lift weights again, I was happy with running as my physical outlet and I ran almost every day. I started with 30-minute runs daily and increased to one hour after two months.

I was amazed to discover that after a run, my brain fog disappeared for a few hours and I could concentrate on my studies. Going for a run was like taking a dose of medicine for my PCS. I would leave my room feeling foggy and depressed, run for an hour, and come back feeling sharp and upbeat. Despite having concussion symptoms that lasted most of the year, my daily running, sometimes twice daily, gave me enough energy and mental focus to do a decent job in my studies. In the end, I was able to finish my first year of university with a low B average. Though it was the lowest average I'd had in a while, I still considered the academic year a success.

Those early transformative experiences with running set the foundation for my running today. In high school, running was the spark that led to losing over 80 pounds and to some great achievements in athletics. In university, running helped me recover from the dark period of dealing with post-concussion syndrome and helped to get my life back on track. Now at 40 years old, with a family and a career, running continues to play a critical role in my life. Running keeps me in shape, gives me great joy, and is my go-to coping mechanism for dealing with life's challenges. Whether my kids are driving me crazy or I've had a bad day at work, my problems always seem smaller after I've gone for a run.

Although I continued running regularly after university, I brought my practice to another level when I discovered ultrarunning. Chance, inspiration, and friendship brought ultrarunning into my life in 2015.

What is Ultrarunning?

The term "ultra" means beyond or on the other side of the marathon distance, and as such, an ultramarathon is any foot race that is longer than the 26.2-mile (42.2-kilometre) marathon. The 100-mile (160 kilometre) race is the main event in ultrarunning and the race typically takes over 24 hours to complete without sleeping. The other common ultradistances include 50 kilometres, 50 miles (80 kilometres), and 100 kilometres. The 200-mile (320-kilometre) race, although more obscure, has started to gain popularity.

Ultramarathons are most commonly run on trails and are held in environments all around the world, including mountains, deserts, and rainforests. Although less numerous than trail races, several ultramarathons take place on indoor and outdoor tracks.

Fastest known times (FKTs), a subset of ultrarunning, have become increasingly popular over the last few years, in large part due to the COVID-19 pandemic. When fewer in-person races were taking place, ultrarunners looked to run their favourite footpaths in record times. Runners record their speed records on the popular website; Fastestknowntime.com.

The Grand Canyon rim-to-rim-to-rim trail in Arizona is perhaps the most popular FKT route for professional ultrarunners. The current FKT is held by top ultrarunner Jim Walmsley who ran the rugged 69-kilometre trail in a blistering 5 hours, 55 minutes in October of 2020. FKTs are discussed in further detail in the aptly named chapter, FKT.

What is Ultraliving?

Ultraliving is a term that I coined to describe the lifestyle that I adopted once I started training for my first ultramarathon. Ultraliving is a holistic practice comprised of mindset, training, and nutrition. Ultraliving practices were at work when I found a way back into ultrarunning in 2017, after almost quitting the sport a year earlier. Ultraliving practices were also present when I documented my performance after every ultramarathon, writing detailed recaps and subsequently using the knowledge to improve.

My Qualifications

I have been running ultramarathons for over six years and have completed all the popular ultramarathon distances. While I'm not an elite ultrarunner, I wouldn't consider myself a mid-pack runner either. I have placed in the top three in three ultramarathons, which included a second-place finish at a 100-mile race in Gatineau, Quebec in 2019. I also currently hold the record for the fastest known time of completing the 138-kilometre Guelph-to-Goderich railway trail without any support. I first started sharing the lessons that I've learned from ultrarunning in October of 2019, when I launched my ultraliving blog; jordanwickett.com. Since then, my blog has attracted thousands of viewers.

Because of my experience being overweight as a child and teenager, I have studied fitness and nutrition for nearly 25 years. In the way of formal education, I have an honours bachelor of science degree, a master of business administration degree, and I completed a personal trainer certificate in 2013. I have also been working in the natural health industry for eight years and have in-depth and specialized knowledge of supplements and natural and organic food. My running experience, education, and life experiences were instrumental in my development of the Ultraliving Lessons.

Why I Wrote This Book

I wrote this book so I can share my ultraliving practices and provide all the tools necessary for a runner to complete their first ultramarathon and subsequent ultramarathons. While running one ultramarathon is difficult, it's even more difficult to stay injury-free while running ultramarathons over a number of years.

The first section, the Ultraliving Lessons, shares stories of my ultrarunning adventures and the major lessons that I've learned from those experiences. The lessons make up the backbone of the ultraliving mindset and focus on themes of motivation, preparation, and perseverance.

The ultraliving mentality is not only applicable to running; this practice will improve one's day-to-day life as well. Dealing with the annoying colleague at work will seem trivial after having to muster up the willpower to run for over 24 hours with aching legs, blistered feet, and an upset stomach. Getting up in the middle of the night to care for a sick child won't seem like a big deal after foregoing sleep altogether and running through the night to complete a 100-mile race.

The second section, the Ultraliving Manual, is a reference guide with all the technical information that a runner needs to complete any ultradistance race. By following the detailed advice on running gear, all the guess work is taken out of building an ultrarunning toolkit. Comprehensive training plans show all the steps necessary to run a 50-kilometre, 50-mile, 100-kilometre, or 100-mile race. Guidance on race day preparation and nutrition is also offered, as well as an overview of the top personalities in the sport. The manual is an encyclopedia for all relevant ultrarunning information.

I am providing a personal guarantee that a beginner can become an accomplished ultrarunner if they take the Ultraliving Lessons to heart and follow the advice in the manual. I've taken over two years to carefully examine my own ultrarunning journey to provide all the tools necessary for a runner to complete their first ultramarathon. Although my book might not change your life, I am certain that ultrarunning will. I sincerely hope that my book inspires you and gives you all the tools that you need to enjoy and embrace this amazing sport.

Part One: The Ultraliving Lessons

Tour du Mont Blanc - August 2008

To my dismay, the scale on the hospital bed registered 240 pounds after I heaved myself onto it. I was presenting the bed to a group of five nurses in a Toronto hospital and I saw smiles and raised eyebrows; the nurses were impressed by the ease of use of the bed's scale and surprised by my weight. Training the staff on hospital beds was a big part of my new marketing associate job with a large medical company. I was proud of my new job; marketing positions were coveted at my company and I worked long hours so I could make a good impression. But I felt the pressure and had slowly put on weight as work got busier.

My job went well for a few months until some personnel changes pushed me to make a change of my own. I felt strongly that I needed to leave my company so I applied to the MBA degree program at the Richard Ivey School of Business (Ivey) at the University of Western Ontario. I worked hard to prepare for the qualifying exam and interview and was delighted to get a thick acceptance package in the mail.

I resigned from my company in early August and had a few weeks off before school started in September. Ivey offered an optional two-week tutorial period before the official start date, but I felt like I didn't need the tutorial since I was a strong student. I decided to use those two weeks for a vacation—

a decision I later regretted because the first few weeks of school were very difficult. Despite the short-term discomfort, I now know that skipping that tutorial period was one of the best decisions of my life. My upcoming trip would spark a lifelong passion.

My first order of business was to ask my wife, Lindsay, for her support with my plans. Lindsay and I had been living together in London, Ontario for three years while Lindsay attended medical school. I had met Lindsay in high school where I was thoroughly impressed by her beauty and many talents. Lindsay has curly brown hair, a heart-shaped face, a great sense of humour, and a caring disposition. I had been riding a high ever since Lindsay and I were married two years earlier. As we are often on the same wavelength, Lindsay recognized the vacation as a great opportunity and gave me her support. Unfortunately, Lindsay couldn't travel with me because of commitments with medical school.

I had resolved to plan a hiking vacation since I loved discovering foreign places on foot. Lindsay and I had travelled to Europe a few years earlier and had spent most of our days walking. We found that we learned more about the cities and sites we visited when we travelled on foot. Through my online research, I found a hiking trip in the French Alps called the Tour du Mont Blanc. The guided tour started in a village in France called Chamonix and went through Italy and Switzerland. I loved the idea of travelling through three different countries on foot. The hike took 10 days and included several overnight stays in small inns called refuges, which were located high in the mountains. I thought about it for a couple of days and then, with a sense of trepidation, booked my trip online.

* * *

I flew into Geneva, Switzerland and took a van for the short ride to Chamonix. I arrived at my hotel midday, dropped off my luggage, and took a walk to explore. I was immediately taken with Chamonix and I wondered how I had never heard of the village before. I enjoyed the delicious smell of fresh bread and coffee as I walked past bakeries and cafes, and I picked up a few last-minute items at one of the mountain equipment stores. I took in the views—French architecture with mansard roofs, town squares, and the snow-capped Mont Blanc towering in the distance. I would later learn that Chamonix is considered the birthplace for a number of extreme sports, including mountaineering and extreme skiing.

That evening, I walked into the small hotel lobby to meet my tour group and joined a group of 10 people who were busily engaged in conversation. We met our tour guide, Gabriel, a young native of Aspen, Colorado, who cracked jokes and made everyone feel comfortable with his informal and welcoming manner. We all took turns introducing ourselves and I took note of the interesting backgrounds. Among our group was a rocket scientist who worked for NASA and a comedy actress from Toronto. Our group was mainly Canadian, but we had a good mix of cultures, with people hailing from Germany, Australia, and Qatar.

We set off into the mountains the next day, everyone carrying heavy packs. I had a big, bulging, green backpack that weighed over 40 pounds. Gabriel pushed the pace and I worked hard to keep up. We hiked up Mont Blanc, on dirt trails and through lush green forests. We crossed a suspension bridge with an amazing view and Gabriel took my photo as I crossed. Our landscape changed as we climbed higher into the mountains, the tree cover thinning and the terrain becoming rockier. We finally reached our destination after six hours of hiking—a quaint, wooden, mountain refuge. I had exerted myself all day on the trails and I loved the way that I felt. I was exhilarated and exhausted.

The days continued with our familiar routine: hiking for around six hours from refuge to refuge, taking in beautiful scenery, having great conversations, and eating delicious food. The mountain refuges were magical places. Our group enjoyed mouth-watering meals, cold beer, wine, and hot coffee, even though we were on the side of a mountain. Some of the mountain refuges were as high as 2,000 metres of altitude.

We hiked through France and then Italy and sampled the food and culture as we went. I could tell that I had lost weight after a few days of hiking. My clothes fit better and I started to use the next notch on my belt. I was surprised because I was eating a lot of food: large meals with extra helpings, snacks, and drinks. Because of my struggles with my weight, I would normally feel anxious about indulging. This was different, though, as I had found a way to enjoy amazing food without the worry of weight gain. I also felt a real sense of calm while I was hiking. Being outside all day and pushing my body felt natural, and the anxiety that accompanied my recent years of working had melted away.

* * *

We crossed back into France on the morning of day 9. Our 10-day trip was coming to an end but there was still another major moment of enlightenment awaiting me. I was hiking with Gabriel when we were passed by two runners going in the opposite direction—a man and woman who were clad in Lycra and wearing small backpacks. We had encountered many fit people on the mountain but these people were different. Our group moved slowly, walking downhill, while this couple easily doubled our pace while going uphill. I had a hard time understanding what I was seeing. I worked hard to keep a decent walking pace on the challenging trails, while this couple ran free and easy.

Gabriel explained that these people were trail runners who were most likely training for a race called the Ultra-Trail du Mont-Blanc (UTMB). The UTMB is a 171-kilometre trail race with over 10,000 metres of vertical gain. It essentially covers the same route that we had hiked, except the average racer completes the whole course in 40 hours. I was shocked that these runners could finish the UTMB trail in less than two days—the same trail that was taking us 10 days to finish.

My first impression was that these runners were crazy and that there was no way I could ever do something like that. Little did I know that I would be lacing up my shoes to run a 100-mile race 10 years later. I didn't decide right away that I wanted to be an ultrarunner, but I knew that I loved spending time on the trails and I loved the sweet feeling of exhaustion at the end of the day. I also loved that I was losing weight while eating a lot—and I mean a lot—of delicious European food. I ended up losing over 10 pounds in the 10 days.

Our tour group returned to the village of Chamonix on day 9 and hiked together one last time on day 10. I was sad to say goodbye to our group; we had grown close through our incredible shared experiences. I reflected on my trip during my van ride back to the airport in Geneva. I had arrived in Chamonix with my life out of whack, stressed and overweight; however, I was going home at peace and in shape. At some point during my hike, I made the profound decision that I must always seek balance in my life and that I needed to use this principle to guide my MBA studies. I didn't have a well-defined plan for my life after the trip, but I knew that I didn't want a career that took over my life.

At the time, I didn't have a plan for running either, yet running would start to become a major part of my life. I never imagined myself as a runner since I've always been a big, strong person who doesn't look like the typical long and lean runner. I certainly didn't think that I would be training for a marathon in a few years, but a marathon attempt was indeed in my future.

Ultraliving Lessons

Get Motivated

I achieved great perspective on my achievements in running after seeing a motivational speaker in 2019. After the speaker delivered an hour of rousing material, he asked everyone to do an exercise in reflection. He told us to note down all the things that we have in our lives today that we didn't think were possible in the past. He went on to ask: Do you live in a house that you never thought you'd be able to afford? Do you have children when you thought that you couldn't have any? Do you have a career that you thought you'd never have? I answered yes to all these questions and came to the important realization that I was taking the significant achievements in my life for granted.

After the event, I reflected on my hiking trip to France 12 years earlier and how much I had achieved with my running. I thought about the awe-inspiring mountain runners and how I didn't think it was possible to achieve their fitness level.

I've found that pinpointing this key moment of motivation has been very helpful when I'm in need of inspiration. When it's hard to wake up early for my run, I remember why I started running in the first place and that gets me out the door.

The Toronto Waterfront Marathon - October 2014

"Screw it. I'm going to quit my job," I said to Lindsay.

I had been working at a multinational consumer goods company for three years and I knew in my heart that I didn't want to stay there. I started working at the company after I finished my MBA program, and although I had made up my mind about leaving, I was still scared. I enjoyed the people I worked with, was making a good salary, and was progressing in my job. I had a plan for my life after leaving my job, but there were still a lot of unknowns and I had never done anything like this before.

Adding to the complex situation, Lindsay was six-months pregnant with our second child. We had welcomed Norah, our beautiful baby girl, into our lives in early 2010. Norah was a delightful, chubby baby and Lindsay and I loved her from the very beginning. Norah was almost bald for the first two years of her life, until she finally sprouted blond ringlet curls. Lindsay and I both have curly hair, but Norah's curls are something to behold. Hers are curls on steroids.

Lindsay was practicing medicine as a family doctor at that point and earning a good income. We had moved to Georgetown, Ontario after Lindsay graduated from medical school and I graduated from my MBA program.

Georgetown is a lovely small town of around 42,000 people and is located a 45-minute drive northwest from Toronto.

Lindsay and I had agreed a few years earlier that I would take time off from work with our second baby since Lindsay had taken the time off with Norah. My original plan was to take a parental leave from my job; however I scrapped those plans after seriously reflecting on my future. Although keeping my job would have been the safe route for my career, I had a dream of starting my own business and I'd had visions of being an entrepreneur since I was a kid. I used to talk about owning a biotechnology company since I studied science in university. I even had a name for my company: Wic Tek, a rearrangement of my last name. Lindsay and I decided that I would resign from my job to look after our children and that I could use my spare time to work on a business idea. My last day of work finally came and I left on good terms. I gave my manager three months of notice, a lot more than usual, so that I could properly transition all my work.

Our son James was born in the summer and Lindsay and I couldn't have been happier. James was a happy and alert baby with beautiful blue-green eyes like his mom's. James's personality shone through early on—a fiery temper paired with a goofball sense of humour. Lindsay took the first three months off work with James and then I took over his care.

Norah was in daycare at that point and James was taking long three-hour naps. I hired a family friend to watch James and to tidy the house for a few hours every day while James slept. I went for runs during those breaks and started to build my endurance. I often ran over a traffic bridge not too far from our house that crossed a wooded ravine and was traversed by a beautiful river. I noticed a gravel trail through the woods in the ravine but I couldn't figure out how to get on the trail.

A few weeks passed and I finally drove around in our car until I found a trailhead for the gravel route in the ravine, and it was only a few minutes from our house. I was immediately taken with my surroundings as I ran the trail for the first time. There was so much to see—large trees swaying in the breeze and groves of ferns growing waist high. I learned from the signs posted just off the gravel footpath that the trail was called Hungry Hollow. I started running Hungry Hollow four to five times per week and developed a profound sense that trail running was the right activity for me. Road running felt like a chore, while trail running conjured up feelings of playing a great childhood game. I enjoyed seeing how fast I could run the small hills, and the trail's twists and turns kept the scenery fresh. While running over Hungry Hollow's three different foot bridges, I enjoyed picturesque views of the emerald-coloured Silver Creek River, with Blue Jays flying, rabbits darting, and, if I was lucky, deer striding.

I had been trail running for a few weeks when our family was invited to a friend's cottage in the Bobcaygeon area north of Toronto. I left the cottage early one morning for my regular one-hour run. I ran 10 kilometres on a gravel road next to the woods and a sparkling lake, and felt so good that I decided to try for another 10 kilometres.

I plodded along happily and eyed my watch—an hour and 15 minutes had passed. The thrill of running in unknown territory kept me going and I ran easily for another 15 minutes. Shortly after, some significant fatigue and knee pain set in but I was determined to continue. The fatigue and sore knees stretched out over the last 30 minutes yet I made it through. I had run for two hours in a row and I felt great about it. I broke a mental barrier and really impressed my wife and our friends when I got back to the cottage.

Later that day, I told Lindsay about my sore knees and she asked me if I had shortened my running stride to deal with the longer distance. She had learned about a shortened stride at some point during her medical career and explained that long strides create a lot of impact on knees and hips. This piece of advice turned out to be one of my most useful tools for running longer distances.

I went for another two-hour run two weeks after my cottage run. The shortened stride felt awkward but I got used to it quickly. I finished the two hours feeling good, without any knee pain. I knew after the run that my shortened stride opened up a whole new set of possibilities for running longer distances. I felt inspired to run a marathon even though I had previously decided that I would never run one. I had seen the pained expressions of the marathon runners at some of the road races I had run. Why would I ever want to put myself through that?

After a small amount of research, I chose the Toronto Waterfront Marathon in October as my first marathon. After that, I needed to come up with a training plan. The race was two months away and I organized my training schedule accordingly. I would run for an hour four times during the week and then do a long run of over an hour on the weekend.

Inspiration ran high during that period of my life and I also began putting some serious work into starting my own business. While James napped, I spent hours brainstorming different ideas and then even more hours evaluating the ideas. In the end, I decided to start a natural men's shaving product business and I called it Naturally Dapper. I spent my weeks looking after James, working on my budding business, and running.

* * *

The late August sun shone brightly on the ravine trail while I went for a run one fateful afternoon. I was halfway through my run when another trail runner caught up to me. I immediately noticed this runner's big brown beard, as it covered his face and descended a few inches below his chin. He was wearing high-quality running gear, which was clearly well used. He introduced himself as Chris and we ran side by side.

Chris asked if I was training for something and I told him about my marathon plans. He told me that he had run the Toronto Waterfront Marathon and that it was a good race. I haphazardly brought up the topic of ultramarathons, recalling my experience in Chamonix. To my surprise, Chris explained that he ran ultramarathons. He had already completed some 100-mile races and was training for another one. Our conversation flowed naturally and I ran with Chris for 20 minutes. We'd only had a brief chat but I could tell that we were going to be friends. We decided to meet for another trail run in a couple of days.

I began running with Chris once or twice per week and I always looked forward to our conversations. Chris told amazing stories about his ultramarathons and I learned that he ran a lot of races with his brother-in-law Joe. In most 100-mile races you can use a pacer since you're running for such a long time. Chris and Joe would often take turns racing and pacing for each other. Chris recounted some of the massive low points that he and Joe had experienced during their 100 milers and how they'd helped each other fight back to finish the races.

I continued to run with Chris as the weeks went by and my marathon got closer. I was learning a lot about running from my conversations with Chris and took note of a goal-setting exercise that he does before all his races. He told me that his number one goal is always to have fun, because why are you spending your free time racing if you're not going to have fun. His number two goal is to finish the race, and his number three goal is to set an aspirational time for finishing the race.

I decided to apply Chris's goal-setting exercise to my upcoming race and was glad that I did, since the exercise relieved some of my nervous energy about the fast-approaching marathon. Setting the goals led me to the realization that I wasn't running to break any records, that going from 10 kilometres to a marathon was a big deal, and that I didn't need to put any extra pressure on myself. My three goals were: (1) to have fun, (2) to finish the race, and (3) to finish the race in under four hours. I was going to treat the race like a fact-finding mission and then I could work on improving my time once I completed one marathon.

The weeks went by and I continued to feel nervous about my upcoming race. I dealt with this nervous energy by going back to my goals. I knew that 42.2 kilometres was a long distance, but I reminded myself that my number one goal was to have fun and that continued to relieve the pressure.

Two weeks out from the marathon, disaster struck. At least, I thought it was a disaster at the time. I developed a fairly intense pain on the outside of my left knee. My mind went to the worst-case scenario and I thought that my knee pain might keep me from finishing the race. I brought it up with Chris on one of our runs and was relieved when Chris shrugged off my concerns. He told me that I had iliotibial (IT) band pain, which is very common for runners. The IT band is a long and thick ligament that runs from your pelvis to your knee along the outside of your leg. Chris explained that I wasn't going to cause any lasting damage from running with a strained IT band and that I should massage my IT band with a foam roller after every run. I bought a foam roller and started using it right away. The rolling worked like a charm and the IT band pain slowly faded after two weeks, just in time for my race.

* * *

My eyes shot open and I glanced at the clock. It was 3:55 a.m. on the day of the marathon and my alarm clock was set to go off at 4:00 a.m. I did a quick mental review of all my training. I had completed about 80 percent of my training plan, which was a very solid effort. One of the things that I love about long-distance running is that there's no way around putting in the work. Someone can't get off the couch and run a marathon on talent alone.

Lindsay and I drove the hour that it took to get downtown and we arrived at the start area an hour and a half before the race. The start line was on

University Avenue, one of the busiest streets in the city. It was amazing to see the street without any cars and filled with people. We arrived early enough for me to warm up and I ran on Queen Street West and then over to the finish line on Bay Street. The 5-kilometre race had started at the beginning of my warm-up and some of the speed demons were already finishing—the winner ran an amazing 16 minutes, 13 seconds.

I warmed up alongside some of the elite Kenyan runners who stuck together in a small group. The Kenyans ran with effortless strides, their feet touching the ground for microseconds as they appeared to hover over the street. Long distance running might be the only sport where amateur runners get to compete with the best runners in the world. For road running and trail running alike, the weekend warriors line up with the elite. I can train as hard as I want for a sport like basketball and never have the chance to play against the likes of LeBron James. Warming up at the same time as the Kenyans felt great, even though I wouldn't be anywhere close to them during the race. I pride myself on arriving early to big life events and it was validating to see that the elite Kenyan runners did the same thing. I wasn't world-class with my running, but I could be world-class with my preparation.

I finished my warm-up, gave Lindsay a big hug, and found my starting corral of runners who were attempting a four-hour marathon. As glamorous as a corral sounds, they serve the important purpose of grouping runners based on estimated finish time. I stood shivering in my single layer of clothes—running tights and T-shirt. I looked around and saw that some of the more experienced runners were wearing garbage bags as jackets, which was a smart move as you can toss the garbage bag in the trash along the course after getting sufficiently warm.

Standing among a sea of 14,734 full-marathon and half-marathon runners, I anxiously awaited the start of the race. Loud music boomed over the PA system as the announcer counted down: five, four, three, two, one. The race started and I ran up University Avenue among the throng of racers. We turned west on Bloor Street and the loud music was replaced with the sound of collective footfalls, reminiscent of rainfall albeit with a slower tempo. Melodic, distinctive, and light. The sound marks the transient moment to commune with fellow runners since the field will spread out quickly after that point. I have run several races since, and the sound of the collective footfalls never fails to make an impression on me.

I ran at my planned pace for the first 10 kilometres as I took in my surroundings. Bands played as I ran by: rock music, Italian music, and steel drums. Spectators held up hilarious signs that covered topics from losing toenails, to hating running, to getting beer at the end of the race. I ran the next 10 kilometres a little over pace since I was enjoying myself, taking extra time at aid stations, and soaking up the atmosphere. I saw Lindsay right around that time which helped to further boost my spirits; it is amazing how seeing your family during a race can perk up your morale. I got back on pace for the next 10 kilometres and completed a respectable split of 3 hours, 5 minutes at the 30-kilometre mark.

I developed some serious cramping in my quads at around 35 kilometres, a new experience for me. I stopped and walked over to the barricades at the side of the street so that I could stretch my quads. I pulled my foot up behind my butt and the stretch eased my quad cramp for about 10 seconds before searing pain shot through the back of my leg and my hamstring seized. I immediately let go of my foot and stood up straight to get rid of the hamstring cramp. The cramp went away but both of my quads then seized and I let out a painful yell. I enacted my display of agony a few feet away from an older spectator and I will never forget her shocked facial expression. She suggested that I stop the race but I was determined to finish. I started running again despite the big knots in my quads.

Fortunately, the pain subsided after 10 minutes of running, when my leg muscles loosened. I could tell that I was getting closer to the finish; the crowds got bigger and a few spectators cheered me on by my name since it was written on my race bib. I got to the final kilometre stretch of the race and realized that I was actually going to finish. I was exhausted but I somehow summoned enough energy to sprint the last 400 metres. The announcer on the PA called out, "Congratulations! Great job, Jordan Wickett," as I ran through the finish line with my arms held high. It was brilliant! I held back tears as I got my medal from the volunteers.

I finished my first marathon in 4 hours, 27 minutes—2,746th out of 3,968 runners. I didn't finish the race in under four hours, but I couldn't have been more proud. I had put in the work for my training, overcome my fears, and completed something big and impactful. I felt like a whole new set of possibilities had opened for me. If I could do something this big, what else could I do?

I felt the afterglow for a whole week. I was really sore and couldn't walk down the stairs without leaning on the banister, yet I still felt great. Shortly after the race, Chris got in touch and wanted to go for a run to talk about my experience, but I was too sore so we had a cup of coffee instead. Chris congratulated me on a successful race and then asked if I had thought about running an ultramarathon. My legs were wrecked after running for over four hours straight. Could I really run for more than that? Chris told me that I could . . . and I believed him.

Ultraliving Lessons

The Three Goals

The Three Goals is an impactful and motivating concept and I'm grateful that Chris shared it with me. Chris is a full-time swim coach and he has led our local swim team, the Halton Hills Blue Fins, for over 13 years. Because of his rich experience working with athletes, Chris has been a great mentor for me. I was very fortunate to randomly meet him on the trails that day in August.

The Three Goals have never failed to keep me motivated for a race over the last six years of ultrarunning. The goals are always:

(1) have fun,

(2) finish the race, and

(3) go for your time.

Setting my top goal as "have fun" reminds me that I'm not a professional runner. Sure, I aspire to continuously improve, but I'm running for recreation and it's supposed to be fun. "Finish the race" reminds me that I need to stick with the race even if I don't reach my time goal. I'll often envision a conversation with Chris when I feel like quitting. Unless I can explain that I'm going to do permanent damage to my body by finishing the race, I know that I don't have an acceptable excuse for Chris. There is also great knowledge gleaned by sticking with your goal until the end. You get valuable first-hand experience on what level of fitness is needed to race the distance effectively. Finally, "go for your time" keeps me focused and in the competitive spirit.

Seven years have passed since my first marathon and I am still struggling with nagging little injuries before races. As I write this section, I have a small hamstring strain that I am working through in preparation for an ultramarathon. The race is four weeks away, which is enough time for my hamstring to heal, but it still worries me. I have learned that I always have nagging little injuries on my mind before a race.

I feel the pressure after signing up for an ultramarathon since I know the race will be challenging and I typically share my plans with my friends and family. I always fear that I won't finish the race and that everyone will know it. As a result, the little ache in my knee can become a major injury in my mind. I know that no one will judge me if I back out of the race because of an injury; however, I've come to recognize these negative thoughts for what they are—fear.

I frequently hear injury stories from aspiring runners. They tell me that they started to run but developed knee pain and decided to stop running as a result. Most new experiences cause fear; it's human nature. New ultrarunners are in uncharted territory because they don't know how the ultradistances will affect their bodies. They have heard the stories about their cousin, aunt, or uncle who blew out their knee because of running. Although there is always a chance of a real injury, it's been my experience that you can train through the small pains. In my six years of ultrarunning, I have never missed an event due to injury.

I am still working on the correct balance of pushing through pain and resting. After all, ultrarunning is an extreme sport. Running 100 miles is not a natural thing for our bodies and it makes sense to be cautious with nagging strains. I often seek advice from Lindsay and Chris for any strains that hang around for two weeks or more. As I get older, I am continuing to work on differentiating between pains that require special attention and those that I can ignore.

La Sauvage - August 2015

I had reached the halfway point on a 1,000-metre descent and was almost sprinting when I tripped and fell hard, letting out a guttural "huh" before I hit the ground. This certainly got the attention of the racers around me and a number of them asked in French if I was alright. I got up quickly and assured everyone that I was okay, even though I wasn't sure—adrenaline had taken over and I couldn't feel much. I was determined to finish the race, though, and I resumed my course down the mountain.

* * *

In the spring of 2015, Lindsay and I decided to spend a month in France with our family in the upcoming summer. We were both still self-employed and wanted to take advantage of it. I had steadily progressed with my small business, Naturally Dapper. I had partnered with a large distributor of natural products in Canada and we got Naturally Dapper into around 200 stores across Canada, including Whole Foods. James had started daycare and I was working on Naturally Dapper full-time. I loved being an entrepreneur and embraced the lifestyle, especially the flexibility in my schedule.

Lindsay and I were funding Naturally Dapper with our own money, which was fine at first but the expenses were adding up quickly. I had made some breakthroughs in the United States, and got Naturally Dapper listed in two large grocery chains. These new customers represented a huge opportunity, but Lindsay and I would need to make another large investment to produce inventory for them. Meanwhile, our existing customers were taking a long time to sell their Naturally Dapper inventory and some of these customers wanted to return their product. The last thing I wanted was to take back a huge order if the product didn't sell through in the United States. Lindsay and I kept a positive attitude about Naturally Dapper but we knew we were at a tipping point.

Running a start-up was stressful and the money concerns were getting to us. We could cut our losses and walk away, or we could find a way to fund the huge amount of inventory needed for the new US customers. Funny enough, a month-long trip to France was our solution to our business concerns and we found a way to fund the trip. We had saved up all our Air Miles and found reasonably priced accommodation through Airbnb. We planned to spend two weeks in the south of France in Nice, 10 days in Cinque Terre in Italy, and then 10 days in the French Alps, ending our visit in Chamonix.

The UTMB race had been in the back of my mind ever since my trip to Chamonix seven years earlier. I wondered if I could run the UTMB someday; the race that inspired me to start trail running. Our trip to France was a great opportunity to gain some mountain running experience and to learn more about UTMB.

We were going to be in Chamonix when the UTMB was taking place, so I looked into running one of the shorter races called the OCC. The UTMB organization puts on four different races at the same time as the 106-mile main event. The OCC is 56 kilometres and its name stands for Orsières-Champex-Chamonix, the names of the main towns along the route. As it turned out, I needed to have registered for the OCC event in December of the previous year. That was disappointing, but I still planned to watch the starts of some of the UTMB races.

I found a shorter mountain race that was not associated with UTMB, called La Sauvage (the Wild) in Pralognan-la-Vanoise (Pralognan), about 130 kilometres south of Chamonix in the French Alps. La Sauvage is 28 kilometres in length through a protected mountainous park, with 1,100 metres of vertical gain and 1,600 metres of descent. This race sounded like a great way to get my first taste of mountain running so I registered for the event and we planned a side trip to the area.

The whole family was excited to embark on our European adventure after so many weeks of planning. Lindsay and I travelled with our two kids, Norah, who was five years old, and James, who was almost three years old. We arrived in Nice on a balmy day in late July. The beautiful azure blue of the ocean was a sight to behold as we flew over Nice's famous Bay of Angels.

After taking a taxi to our accommodations, we took the rest of the day to get our bearings and purchase some groceries. We got busy exploring the city the next day and visited the rocky beach and the markets. We ate ice cream while walking the old streets and went for a long stroll on the beachside walkway called Promenade des Anglais. Feeling tired yet enriched, we returned to our Airbnb rental to make dinner.

We followed a similar routine for the rest of our visit in Nice. We walked for hours on the Promenade, beside the rows of blue-and-white-striped beach umbrellas. There was a lot to do in Nice, but it wasn't the best place for kids. We got the sense that our kids weren't appreciated in most places and there weren't many young families around. As a result, we were ready to leave Nice when it was time to board our train to Cinque Terre in Italy.

Cinque Terre means "five lands" in Italian and is named for the five coastal villages that are grouped closely together. The villages are beautiful, with pastel-coloured buildings built into rugged oceanside mountains. Contrary to Nice, the people in Cinque Terre were much more relaxed about kids and we felt welcome and at ease with our family. We spent most of our time at a small beach near the apartment we rented and exploring the villages. I was sad to leave Cinque Terre after our 10-day visit, but was excited to get into the mountains of France.

We got back on the train and headed north to Annecy, France, which is set on a lake and surrounded by mountains. We settled in nicely in Annecy and enjoyed going for long bike rides around the lake. Our week-long visit went by quickly in this picturesque medieval town. The day before my trail race, we picked up a rental car in Annecy and drove it through the French Alps to Pralognan. We drove on a spectacularly clear and sunny day and were awestruck by the amazing views of the mountains. We arrived in the small alpine town of Pralognan in the afternoon and after checking in to our hotel,

I got all my trail running gear organized and went to bed feeling excited and nervous about the race.

I got up early on race day and walked over to the city hall for our 6:45 a.m. pre-race briefing. Shortly after, just over 140 racers were bussed to a ski resort town called Tignes. In Tignes, we were directed to the start line at the base of a mountain. The big mountains were intimidating and I didn't know how I would fare on the challenging terrain. The race director counted down from 10 and we were all off, running up the mountain. Like the start of the Toronto Marathon, the sounds of all the runners grouped together made an impression on me. Watches beeping, water sloshing in hydration packs, and the collective sound of footfalls.

We ran uphill on switchbacks and I worked hard to keep up. Fortunately, most runners started walking after five minutes. I slowed down to a fast hike and kept up with the main part of the pack. I took special note of a big guy who passed me and continued to pass runners in the early part of the race. He looked like he weighed around 240 pounds, like how I looked before I got in shape. I was certain that I would be passing this big guy later in the race when he ran out of energy.

I reached the top of the climb at 2,700 metres and ran for about five minutes. I hit the first aid station and couldn't believe my eyes. An amazing spread was laid out before me, including fine chocolate, two kinds of raisins, prunes, peanuts, crackers, and gummy bears. I was also offered hot tea and soup. The French really know how to stock an aid station.

A short time after leaving the aid station, I increased my pace and passed a few racers before arriving at the halfway point. Although mountain running was new to me, I was gaining confidence with every runner that I passed. At that point, I had become very hot from running in the jacket I had worn since the beginning of the race. I was making such great progress, though, that I didn't want to stop to take the jacket off. What's more, I had the big guy in my sights. With much satisfaction, I passed the big guy shortly after the halfway mark.

Maintaining a strong pace, I reached the last aid station and had a quick drink of water. I only had eight kilometres to go over a descent of 1,000 metres. Feeling good, I descended fast and passed a few more people. In a short period of time, my attitude had changed from feeling nervous to overconfident. Sensing the finish line, I ran even faster, even though I was on a particularly steep section. I caught my foot on a rock and fell hard. Getting the attention of the runners around me, I let out a grunt as I hit the ground and created a big cloud of dust. Dying from embarrassment, I got up quickly and continued running. I had no idea if I had injured myself, but I was getting the hell out of there. I ran for a few more minutes and quickly assessed my body as the adrenaline died down. It turned out that I was okay but I had scraped my knee and sprained my thumb. I slowed down to avoid another fall and a few runners passed me, including the big guy. I was disappointed but I knew that I was still running a good race.

I finished the last part of the descent and ran into Pralognan where I was greeted by a small cheering crowd. I felt amazing crossing the finish line, even with blood running down my leg from the knee scrape. I was thrilled to hear "Daddy" and to see Lindsay, Norah, and James waiting for me.

I finished in 3 hours, 53 minutes, which was much faster than my expected 4 hours, 40 minutes. Lindsay said that she suspected that I might finish early and she wanted to make sure that she was there. I finished 79th out of 141 finishers.

We enjoyed some more of the aid-station food before leaving, including sparkling water, banana bread, orange bread, and a selection of cheeses. We stopped at a grocery store on the way back to our hotel and stocked up on some more French food for a little celebration back at our room.

The next day we drove our rental car to Chamonix and checked in to a quaint little wooden cottage in Les Houches, a village at the base of Mont Blanc. We had arrived on the weekend before the start of UTMB week. Lindsay and I splurged on a nice dinner for the family at a traditional French restaurant in Les Houches on our first night. We were all soaking in the ambience, candlelight, amazing aromas, and people speaking several different languages. Norah and James, who usually had a hard time sitting down for dinner at restaurants, were on their best behaviour. Lindsay and I split a cheese fondue and a nice bottle of French wine. We both agreed that this meal was a great way to kick off our visit to Chamonix.

The following day we walked around the village of Chamonix and took in the UTMB atmosphere. We visited the outdoor trade show and walked over to the start line to take some pictures. I was disappointed that we were going to miss the main race; however, we needed to get back home for Norah and

James's first day of school. Our only flight option left on the Friday, which was the same day as the main UTMB event.

The Petite Trotte à Léon (PTL), another UTMB event, starts on the Monday of race week. PTL is a 300-kilometre event with 25,000 metres of elevation and teams of three run the race together. I woke up early on Monday and drove to the village so that I could watch the PTL start at 8:00 a.m. I made my way among the hundreds of spectators to the Place du Triangle de l'Amitié, the iconic village square where the UMTB main event starts and finishes. I climbed up on a planter to improve my view just as it started to pour rain. True to form for ultrarunners, the rain didn't faze any of the racers. They stood in place, stoic, as the dramatic music started from the PA system. A voice came on the PA and sent the runners off as the instrumental music built to a crescendo. Around half of the runners ran and the other half walked. Despite not sprinting away from the start like the runners of the main event, I could tell the participants were excited by the looks on their faces. Looks of joy and pride mixed with nervousness. They were off on an amazing adventure. The rain, the music, and the setting all made for a moving experience. I was inspired more than ever to come back to UTMB someday.

We arrived back home in early September, just before the first day of school, after spending five weeks in Europe, the longest vacation we'd ever taken. I felt anxious about having taken so much time off and was glad to be back to a normal routine. The trip was extremely valuable, though, and accomplished what we intended. We were back at home in what seemed like our old lives, but we had made some big changes. During our trip, Lindsay and I had in-depth conversations about Naturally Dapper and concluded that it was time to wind up our start-up business. We decided that I'd look for a more traditional job in the same industry and I could use the business contacts that I'd made while working on Naturally Dapper. I had also gained a lot of confidence as a mountain runner and felt inspired once more by UTMB in Chamonix. Perhaps the biggest benefit of all from the trip was unintended. Lindsay surprised me with some big news shortly after we got back home. Shutting down Naturally Dapper wasn't going to be our only major life change . . .

Ultraliving Lessons

You Don't Need a Runner's Body to Run

I was very focused on my weight during that time of my life. I was proud of the way that I looked yet I was fixated on my diet. I had reasoned that the skinnier I became, the better I would get at running. My perception changed, however, when the big guy beat me in La Sauvage. He taught me that I don't need to have the perfect runner's body to run well on trails. Sure, I want to be in the best shape possible, but I don't need to wait until I am in perfect shape.

There is No Substitute for Action

I was legitimately surprised at how well I raced La Sauvage. I didn't expect to beat any serious mountain runners or to get my finish time. I finished the race with a lot of confidence and that came from the action of actually doing the race. I could have continued to plan and to reflect on what was needed to eventually run UTMB, but that would only have taken me so far. The action of running a mountain race gave me some very valuable insights and a strong foundation for my next races.

50 Miles on the Bruce Trail - November 2015

A few days after we got back from France, Lindsay joined me in the kitchen as I was making breakfast. She was smiling and carried something small in her hand. She revealed a pregnancy test and showed me the faint line. I didn't make the connection at first and Lindsay had to explain that she was pregnant again. Similar to my reaction with our first two children, I didn't believe it. The line on the pregnancy test was so faint. Could it really be the case? I quickly came around to realizing that we were going to be parents again. Another big change; however, this was great news. Lindsay and I had been trying for another baby for a long time without success. Discouraged, we took a break from trying before we left for France. We weren't trying for a pregnancy while we were in France, but we did some much-needed relaxing that proved to be the magic ingredient. We felt cautiously optimistic, since we'd had some very tough experiences with lost pregnancies during the last few years. We knew that we needed to get past the 12-week mark for Lindsay to have a strong chance at carrying the pregnancy to term.

    I was shutting down Naturally Dapper, looking for a new job, and we had a third child on the way. There was only one thing to do—run. Running helped me stay organized and gave me something to look forward to. I loved my daily training sessions; they lifted my mood and kept me in good shape. I had some great momentum with my running achievements and I wanted to keep it going. I decided to run the Scotiabank Toronto Waterfront Marathon again in mid-October and finished in a solid 3 hours, 54 minutes, taking 33 minutes off my previous time. I felt confident and was eager to explore the longer ultramarathon distances. I started looking for local races that I could run before the end of the year, but it was late in the season and I couldn't find anything over 50 kilometres until the spring.

I shared my running aspirations with Chris when we were out for a run one day, a week after the 2015 Toronto Marathon. Chris suggested that we do our own 50-mile trek on the Bruce Trail. At 890 kilometres, the Bruce Trail is the longest footpath in Canada. Established in 1967, the trail starts in the Niagara region and runs all the way through to Tobermory. The trail follows the Niagara escarpment, the rock formation that Niagara Falls flows over. The escarpment has a lot of variety in terrain, with undulating hills, rocks, and mud. Chris and I loved the idea and made plans to go for our trek on a Saturday in early November.

We invited Chris's brother-in-law Joe on our trek since Joe is a strong runner with a great attitude. What's more, Joe had strong knowledge of the local Bruce Trail routes and offered to plan our 50-mile trek. We gratefully took Joe up on his offer and he planned an out-and-back trek for us from Georgetown to the Forks of the Credit Provincial Park near Orangeville.

Our 50-mile trek was a week away and I started feeling anxious about it. I knew that I would be on the trails for an entire day and I had family obligations. I was also worried about the cold November weather. I called Chris to share my doubts, secretly hoping that he had similar reservations about the trek. Chris assured me that we were going to have a great time and that I was up for the challenge. I had been progressing well with my training and he was sure I could run the 50 miles. His enthusiasm for our trek was great to hear and I fed off that energy, feeling much better about our planned run.

Our Bruce Trail trek started at 6:00 a.m. on a frosty Sunday morning in early November. Joe met me at a trailhead around 10 kilometres west of Georgetown while it was pitch dark. We left our cars and set off on what was sure to be an adventure. Joe led the way on the trail and set a good pace. We chatted as we went while also taking time to enjoy the silence, which was remarkable at that time of year. Joe is about 10 years younger than me, yet we became fast friends despite the age gap. I had gotten to know Joe by joining Chris and Joe on several of their training runs. Joe had been running ultramarathons for a few years and had completed a number of 100-mile races. I was inspired by Joe's running since we have similar builds— we are both tall with big frames and we do not look like your average runner.

It was silent and still when the sun peeked over the horizon; we could only hear our breath and the crunch of our feet on frozen grass. Joe and I were crossing a farmer's field that had a light mist hanging above it. The sunrise made the mist glow and gave the impression of a magical landscape. I have witnessed many sunrises since, and I always take time to appreciate their beauty and the associated positive feelings of affirmation, joy, and thoughtfulness.

Joe and I covered 30 kilometres at a good pace as we ran into Terra Cotta, a beautiful small town north of Georgetown. We met Chris there, who planned to join us for the remaining 50 kilometres. We had lunch with Chris and then got back to running on muddy trails—the ground had thawed and was slowing us down. We watched our footing as we descended a 200-metre cliff into Belfountain, just outside of the Forks of the Credit Provincial Park. That section is both beautiful and challenging, having one of the highest elevations on the Bruce Trail. We ran through Belfountain and then passed through a small village called Brimstone. Brimstone has a great sign posted at its entrance: "Once home to several hundred hard living quarry men 1880s–1910s."

We arrived at the Forks of the Credit Provincial Park shortly after Brimstone. The park is a beautiful area with rolling hills and great views of the Credit River. We spent around two hours running in the park and were treated to views of an amazing sunset.

Forks of the Credit marked the halfway point for our trek. Since we were doing an out-and-back trip, we reluctantly left the park and started our journey homeward. Backtracking, we climbed the cliff out of Belfountain in the dark. Once we reached the top of the cliff, we startled a family whose house backed on to the trail. The family had been unpacking groceries from their van as we ran by with our headlamps on. I can only imagine their surprise from seeing three grown men running in the dark in November.

We had covered 60 kilometres at that point, which was the farthest that I had ever run. I was starting to feel tired and shared this with Chris and Joe. Joe had brought something that he called a coconut bomb, a mixture of coconut sugar, coconut butter, and coconut oil. Chris and Joe both follow strict plant-based diets and they were experts at fueling with everything vegan. Joe had put the coconut bombs in a little plastic baggie so that I could tear the end off and push the mixture through the bag into my mouth. Joe said that the fats in the coconut bomb would help with my energy level. He warned that the coconut bomb would make me feel sick for a little while, probably 20 minutes, but that I would then start feeling better. I wasn't keen on feeling sick to my stomach, but I was open to Joe's advice. Funnily enough, I would get the same sort of advice from Joe about a year later during an important race.

I ate the coconut bomb and just like Joe said, I started feeling sick to my stomach. It lasted for about 15 minutes and then I got a significant energy boost. This was my first experience with the importance of nutrition during a race. I took special note of how the rush of calories renewed my energy levels and lifted my mood.

We had around 20 kilometres left when we came to the top of a hill near the Cheltenham Badlands, a popular area with rolling hills of bare red earth. The sky was clear, and at our elevation, we had an amazing view of the city lights of the Greater Toronto Area. We took a moment to appreciate the view and then continued over a short stretch of road. The three of us ran side by side and we picked up the pace as we got closer to home. Reaching the end of a road section, we turned on to forested single track. We ran our last few miles through the cold and dark and I got some great encouragement from my friends. Chris and Joe were already experienced ultrarunners and they were excited that I was about to finish my first ultradistance trek. We finally got back to where Joe and I had started earlier that day; it had taken us over 12 hours. We all exchanged hugs and high fives. At long last, we were done. I was exhausted, sore, and cold, but I was an official ultrarunner.

A week or two after the trek, Lindsay visited a prenatal clinic in nearby Brampton for an ultrasound. We were at the critical 12-week mark with Lindsay's pregnancy and we were going to the clinic to confirm that the pregnancy was viable. I looked after Norah and James while Lindsay got called into one of the examination rooms. I kept it cool for the sake of the kids, but

I was a nervous wreck inside. The kids must have picked up on my energy because they started running in circles inside the waiting room. I promptly took Norah and James for a walk outside to relieve some anxiety.

Spending 15 minutes outside served its purpose. Norah, James, and I felt calmer as we re-entered the clinic. We got called into the examination room with Lindsay shortly after our walk. I entered the room to see Lindsay lying on her back and an unrecognizable image on the ultrasound machine. We were shown a fluttering on the screen, one that looked like a small butterfly flapping its wings. I made eye contact with Lindsay and noticed the serene smile on her face. We were seeing our baby's heartbeat. Lindsay and the ultrasound technician explained that we had a very good chance of carrying our pregnancy to term since we were at the 12-week mark with a strong heartbeat. I held back tears. That little fluttering was one of the best sights that I've ever seen.

Naturally, Lindsay and I started planning for the eventual arrival of our next baby. We arranged for Norah and James to move into the same room so that the baby could have a nursery. Alongside plans for the baby, I was making plans for running. I signed up for an ultramarathon in the spring and was expecting great results. After all, I had completed La Sauvage and the Bruce Trail trek without any major difficulties. The next race wouldn't go quite as smooth, though, and I was about to learn a hard lesson about ultrarunning.

Ultraliving Lessons

Get a Running Partner

I nearly backed out of my 50-mile Bruce Trail trek because I was afraid. I was scared that the trek would take too much time away from my family and that it would be too cold on the trails. Fortunately, Chris recognized my fear and quashed it. Chris had successfully completed several ultramarathons and knew what to expect from a 50-mile trek. He knew that my family would support my trek and that we could handle the cold weather.

I realized during this experience what a huge benefit it is to have a running partner. To this day, fear creeps in before running events and I often look for reasons to back out on my commitments. Fortunately I have a sounding board with Chris, who keeps me grounded and accountable.

It's not always easy to find a running partner and I was very fortunate to meet Chris randomly on the trails in Georgetown. In addition to Chris, I often turn to social media for support since many trail runners post about their training and racing on Instagram. Over the years, I've developed a group of hundreds of supporters on Instagram and I exchange likes and encouraging messages with these friends on a daily basis.

Sulphur Springs 50 km (Part 1) - May 2016

I didn't stick around after the race, even though I had left all my gear in Joe's tent. I wanted to get home to talk to Lindsay and I couldn't help replaying the race in my mind. Where had I gone wrong? Sulphur Springs 50 km certainly hadn't gone according to plan and I was dealing with the aftermath.

* * *

My professional life was still in flux in the winter of 2016 but the dust was settling. Lindsay and I had successfully wound up Naturally Dapper and I had started a new job in sales in February with a supplement company based in the west coast of Canada. I hit the ground running with that job since I could use a lot of the contacts I had made from Naturally Dapper.

I was on a roll with my running and felt confident when I signed up for a 50-kilometre race called Sulphur Springs. Sulphur Springs is a trail race in the Dundas Valley Conservation Area, just outside of Hamilton, Ontario. It's one of the largest trail races in Canada and it has a number of ultradistances: 50 kilometres to 100 miles. Chris encouraged me to do the 50 miler since I had already completed our trek, but I decided to start with 50 kilometres so that I could ease into ultraracing. This proved to be a very good decision since I was destined to hit a major obstacle at Sulphur Springs.

I had put together a training plan and I ran through the tail end of the winter months and into spring. My running felt strong and I consistently built distance with my long runs. Having already run 50 miles, I figured that the 50-kilometre distance was going to be a breeze. I ran mainly in the mornings while it was cool, with temperatures at around 10°C–15° C. I figured that I would be running the race in similar temperatures, but I couldn't have been more wrong.

* * *

David didn't wail when he came into the world in the late spring. The doctors thought he looked healthy but were concerned that he wasn't crying. David was just showing his personality, though, as he was a very relaxed baby. I breathed a sigh of relief when David eventually started crying when he was weighed and checked. The hospital staff passed him back to Lindsay so that David could rest on her chest. Our whole family instantly fell in love with David. He was smothered with kisses and hugs from Norah and James, and he was constantly being snuggled by either Lindsay or me.

David thrived as a baby, putting on weight and eating well. I helped with the family, worked at my new job, and I ran. Lindsay and I somehow kept everything together; this was our third baby and we knew what to do.

Before I knew it, Sulphur Springs was a few weeks away. It didn't even cross my mind that I should consider postponing the race since life was so busy. Lindsay had always been supportive of my running and she knew that I was really looking forward to Sulphur Springs. She supported my plan of camping with Chris and Joe on the Friday night before the race and then running on Saturday morning.

Chris and Joe got to the race site just after noon on the Friday before the race and set up Joe's family-sized tent. Joe's tent was like a small cottage; you could stand up straight while inside and it could easily sleep three grown men on cots. They set up the tent in an open field near the start/finish area. The Sulphur course is a 20-kilometre loop with a respectable 620 metres of elevation. Chris and Joe had run Sulphur before and told me that it was great to have a base camp with all your gear at the start/finish. I worked the full day on Friday and then rushed over to the race just before dark.

I didn't feel very well rested when I woke up at 4:30 a.m. the next day. It had taken me a while to calm down the night before after rushing to the race. I shook it off, though, and made my coffee and breakfast. I noticed that Chris and Joe started drinking water right after they woke up. I should have done the same, but I continued drinking my coffee instead. I was only running 50 kilometres after all.

I watched Chris and Joe start their races at 6:00 a.m. since my race started at 7:00 a.m. Chris was running the 50 miler and Joe was running the 100 miler. The energy was palpable as the races started and I felt a pang of regret that I wasn't running with them. When it was my turn to run, I gathered my gear and went to line up a little ways down from the start. The race director counted down to send us off and it was my turn to share in the energy of the start line. I was off and running fast—close to my road marathon pace. It was 7:00 a.m. and still fairly cool and I ran the first 10-kilometre loop in just over 56 minutes, a speedy pace for a hilly course. I felt great as I came back to the start/finish area.

I continued my fast pace as I left for my first 20-kilometre loop—I had two 20-kilometre loops left. I ran another 10 kilometres quickly and made a brief stop at the aid station to refill my water. I carried two 500 millilitre hand-held bottles and only refilled one of them since I didn't want to waste time at the aid station. Though it was around 9:00 a.m., it was getting hot. I did myself a big disservice by not drinking more water but I didn't realize it at the time.

I came back into the start/finish area a little before 10:30 a.m. I finished my first 20-kilometre loop in a fast 2 hours, 26 minutes. The heat was in full force at this point; it was 28°C and I was sweating profusely. My clothes were drenched and sweat poured down my legs, soaking my shoes and socks. I had used Band-Aids to cover my nipples to prevent chafing but I was so sweaty that the Band-Aids fell off. Perhaps it sounds like a small thing; however, nipple chafing can ruin your day pretty quickly during a race. I was bleeding through my shirt and when I tried to re-apply Band-Aids to my nipples, they simply fell off since I was too sweaty. I decided to run without a shirt, which made me really uncomfortable as I'm self-conscious because of my previous challenges with my weight.

I soldiered on and kept a good pace as the temperature rose to a steamy 34°C. I had filled both of my water bottles at the start/finish, but I drank them quickly and ran for around 30 minutes without water. Coming into the first aid station, around eight kilometres on the course, I spent some time drinking additional water and refilling my water bottles. I didn't take any electrolytes, though, and I was only getting salt from the gels that I had been eating every

45 minutes. I felt good leaving the aid station but soon slowed down as I reached open trail, the sun beating down on me. I had a massive bonk at this point and needed to walk. Bonking is runner speak for completely running out of energy. Feeling terrible, I stepped into the woods for a pee. I noticed my stream was a weird colour and was horrified when I realized that I was peeing blood. I thought about calling the emergency phone number so that race staff could come pick me up, but I only had eight kilometres left. I decided to do an easy walk to the finish line since I didn't want to wait around.

I trudged across the finish line to a small round of applause, but I didn't feel like smiling. I had finished the race mid-pack with a time of 6 hours, 49 minutes. I immediately walked over to the paramedic who was a friendly young guy. I explained my woes and was surprised by his response.

"Can you produce some of this bloody piss for me?" said the paramedic.

This was a strange request but I cooperated. I got a paper cup, walked to a porta-potty, and returned with my bloody urine. The paramedic confirmed that it was bloody urine and told me I couldn't go back on the course. When he asked me to turn around and he started to poke my kidneys, wanting to know if it was painful, I realized that I wasn't working with the brightest paramedic. He gave me a small punch in one of my kidneys as the last part of his examination. Fortunately, my kidneys weren't sore to the touch and the paramedic ended our chat by telling me that I should go to the emergency department at the nearest hospital.

I called Lindsay for advice since I knew I would be in for a long wait at the emergency department. I tried Lindsay a few times but couldn't get through, so I called my sister Jamie who is also a family doctor. I got through to Jamie and, jokingly, she told me that I'm crazy to run these races but assured me that I wasn't going to die. She told me to stop and get a big bottle of water and to have it with some chips so that I could get some salt. I got in my car and stopped at the first gas station that I saw. I picked up a two-litre bottle of water and a large bag of chips and promptly consumed all of it.

Getting home 45 minutes later, I was very relieved to see that my urine was back to normal. Lindsay was home and she recommended that I continue to drink water and monitor the colour of my pee. She said that I didn't need to go to the hospital if I didn't have any more blood in my stream. I also spoke to my brother-in-law who is a doctor in Ottawa—we have a lot of doctors in our family! He had seen a runner that same day peeing blood after the Ottawa

Marathon. This runner went into kidney failure shortly after the run and suffered some serious health consequences. This news sent me into a spiral of worry about ultrarunning. I loved running and pushing myself, but I certainly didn't want to do any lasting damage to my body. I had a family to support and finishing ultras seemed like a silly reason for putting my family's welfare at risk.

I checked in with Chris and Joe the next day. Chris had a good showing with 9 hours, 47 minutes for his 50 miler, finishing in 15th place out of 109 racers. Joe had a tough time, completing 120 kilometres of his 100 miler (160 kilometres) before dropping out. Chris asked me when we were going to race again and I told him that I was taking a break. I didn't mention how much ultrarunning now scared me. I didn't know if I'd ever run another race.

Ultraliving Lessons

Distance Progression

A lot went wrong with Sulphur Springs, but one thing that I got right was running 50 kilometres instead of jumping up to 50 miles or 100 miles. Bryon Powell, the author of the ultrarunning bible *Relentless Forward Progress: A Guide to Running Ultramarathons*, recommends building your race distances slowly and taking time to appreciate all of them. This is sage advice for running and life, since it takes time to become proficient at an activity. Babies need to master walking before they can run. Students need to finish high school before they can go to university. If I had started racing at the 50-mile distance I might have been tempted to push through the dehydration and could have done some serious harm. I had a lot to learn about ultrarunning and keeping the distance to 50 kilometres kept me from making a big mistake.

Race Reports

It is common practice among runners to reflect on running events with a written race report. In race reports, runners typically review what went well, what had gone wrong, and potential improvements. On one of my many training runs with Chris, he had mentioned that he writes a race report after most of his ultramarathons.

I took some time to write a race report shortly after Sulphur Springs. I wrote about the errors with my hydration—not taking enough salt or drinking enough water. I didn't have a good solution for nipple chafing, which forced me to run without a shirt. There is conflicting research, but I believe that running without a wet shirt to cool me down made me sweat even more. I also got to the race late on Friday night and felt tired and flustered on race day as a result. Maybe I would have made better decisions during the race if I was more rested. Finally, I ran at maximum effort in sweltering temperatures after not having trained in the heat.

I felt a lot better about Sulphur Springs after writing my race report and getting a better understanding of what went wrong. My extreme dehydration wasn't an anomaly; I knew what factors led to it. Writing the recap also helped me sort out my feelings about the race—disappointment, shame, and fear. I still didn't know if I would ever race again; however, the race report process helped me make some peace with the situation.

Haliburton Forest 50 Miler - September 2017

I pushed send on my text message to Chris, politely declining his offer to join him for a trail run. I hadn't run in a month, ever since Sulphur Springs. I didn't share with Chris that I was still scared that I might hurt my kidneys again if I pushed myself. I was also ashamed of messing up a 50-kilometre race after I had trained so much. At that point, running felt like the meal that you eat before throwing up—you avoid the meal for a long time afterwards. I had started cycling and swimming to take the place of running. After a few weeks, I felt the familiar urge to run, but I suppressed it. I still needed some distance from running.

    I discussed my feelings about Sulphur Springs with Lindsay during this break from running. A natural healer, Lindsay helped me sort through my emotions and fears. Another two months went by before I warily laced up my shoes for a short trail run on a sunny day in early August. I ran at an easy pace for 20 minutes and constantly monitored my body for pain. To my great relief, I felt good after the run and, most importantly, I didn't pee blood afterwards. I slowly started building distance on the trails as the weeks passed. Twenty minutes of running became half an hour, which then became an hour.

I gained confidence with every training run but I still didn't have any plans to race. Life went on and I busied myself with parenting and my career. I kept up a good level of running and gained even more confidence as we moved into the spring. Almost a full year had passed since Sulphur Springs, when I met Chris for a trail run on a beautiful sunny day in May. When Chris asked if I was planning any races, I finally shared that I was still gun-shy from Sulphur Springs. Chris explained that peeing blood, although dangerous, is fairly common in ultrarunning. I didn't know that our mutual friend, who is an accomplished ultrarunner, had a similar experience at Sulphur Springs. Chris explained that our friend had to drop out of the race because he was peeing blood; however, he went on to finish a number of other 100-mile races that same season. Chris assured me that I was fine and encouraged me to run a nearby race, called the Haliburton Forest Trail Race, in the fall.

I let the conversation with Chris simmer for a couple of days and then gathered up my nerve to register for the 50-mile distance at Haliburton Forest. The race would take place in mid-September and I had five months to get ready. Having a race in my calendar felt great, yet I was still nervous about hydration. I spoke to Chris about his hydration strategy before I attempted my first major long run in my training plan. Chris stressed the importance of salt pills and explained that he takes one to two pills every 45 minutes during a race. As always, I was grateful for Chris's advice and planned to test out salt pills on my upcoming four-hour training run.

I often listen to podcasts while I run and my favourite is Ethan Newberry's *Ginger Runner Live*. Ethan and his wife, Kim, have been interviewing top ultrarunners for years. Over the dozens of *Ginger Runner* podcasts that I've listened to, I noticed that many runners recommend practicing your nutrition before your race, so that way you can be certain your nutrition won't make you sick on race day.

Taking this advice to heart, I tested out salt pills for the first time on a four-hour training run during a hot day in July. Like Chris had recommended, I took one to two salt pills every 45 minutes and was amazed with my results. I fought off dehydration and avoided any major muscle cramping.

The months went by and I slowly made my way through my training plan. I was pleased with my progress and I gradually increased my mileage. After countless hours of training, the time had finally come to run the Haliburton

Forest 50 Miler. I was glad to have that old feeling back. I was excited to race again.

I took the day off from work before the race and drove to Haliburton Forest with Chris and Joe. Joe was running the 100 miler and Chris was going to crew for us. Haliburton Forest is a beautiful wooded park in Ontario's cottage country. I was surprised to learn that Haliburton Forest has its own wolf pack that has lived in 15 acres of protected forest since 1993. We arrived at the race site mid-afternoon and chose a campsite near the start/finish area. We set up Joe's big tent, had some supper and a beer, and then got to bed early.

I woke up at 4:00 a.m. the next morning and immediately got started on my hydration, taking a salt pill with some water. Joe and I had breakfast, gathered our gear, and walked over to the start line. The 100-mile and 50-mile races both started at 5:00 a.m. and Joe and I had decided that we would run together for as long as possible. I felt great as I lined up at the start line; I was racing with an experienced ultrarunner and the weather was a cool 10°C. The race director counted down from 10 and started the race. The front of the pack went out quickly and I was tempted to keep up with them, but Joe held us back. He said that it was important to stick to our pace and we would pass a number of the runners later on in the race.

The Haliburton Forest course is a 50-mile loop system on mostly single track. The trails run alongside small lakes that are interspersed throughout the course, making for great views. Joe and I made steady progress during the first part of the race and the hours went by quickly. We were enjoying each other's company, chatting, and reminding each other to eat gels and to take salt pills.

We had been running for over five hours when we met Chris at the halfway-point aid station. We were happy to see Chris and we devoured the avocado and hummus wraps that he brought us. Chris told me that I looked good and I told him that I felt good. I was doing a good job on my hydration and I was in good spirits. Chris cheered us on as we left the aid station, urging us to go hard for the rest of the race.

We continued at a good pace for another three hours until Joe's quads became painful. He needed to slow down and suggested that I go ahead without him. I reluctantly left Joe since I only had around 15 kilometres left and I wanted to continue pushing myself. Shortly after leaving Joe, I encountered a group of Scouts Canada hikers on a technical section of trail. I turned on the jets so that I could move past them and I heard a few of the Scouts remark on how fast I was going. I was encouraged by these compliments and felt great that I was moving so well after 10 hours on the trail. Joe's plan had paid off for me since I had conserved energy from managing my pace earlier on in the race.

The finish line finally came into sight after I had run for another hour. I was so excited and envisioned getting my race medal and drinking a cold beer; however, my heart sank as I saw a set of course signs. The signs directed me onto a winding trail through the woods and I realized that the race wasn't over yet.

I finally made it through the last trail and then mustered the energy to run hard to the finish. Chris was there cheering me on and I held back tears as I crossed the finish line. I felt an amazing sense of accomplishment. I'd gone from thinking that I'd never run an ultramarathon again to completing a challenging 50-mile race without any major difficulties. I had finished in 11 hours, 48 minutes and in 31st place out of 54 racers.

Chris and I set up chairs near the finish line to wait for Joe and I got to enjoy my cold beer. We watched a few of the 100-mile racers come in and turn right back around to start their second 50-mile loop. I told Chris that with the way I was feeling, there was no way that I would go back out for another loop. However, after eating dinner and having 30 minutes of rest, I felt like I could go back on the course if I needed to. A little bit of rest, food, and company is a powerful thing during an ultramarathon.

Joe arrived at our campsite an hour after I had finished, with a limp and a grave look on his face. He explained that his quad pain had worsened and that he was going to drop out of the race. Chris and I encouraged Joe to go back out but Joe was set on dropping. Although I felt bad for Joe, I could sympathize with his decision. Joe was facing the daunting task of starting another 50 miles of running after reaching the potential comforts of his tent, a hot shower, and a full night's sleep.

We decided to stay the night in Haliburton Forest since it was late and we didn't feel like packing up all of our gear in the dark. I slept well but awoke to the wolves howling during the night. I imagined how it would feel to be one of the 100-mile runners hearing the wolves and running on the trails in the pitch dark.

We had breakfast in the Haliburton Forest restaurant the next morning, each ordering coffee and a big plate of hash browns, the only plant-based option on the menu. I follow suit and eat vegan meals when I'm with Chris and Joe. I told them that I was going to take the next step and sign up for a 100-kilometre race. After all, it was only 20 kilometres longer than the 50-mile (80-kilometre) race that I had just run. Chris and Joe nodded their heads.

"You should run the Sulphur Springs 100 kilometre race," said Chris.

I winced at this suggestion since Sulphur Springs was such a bad experience for me. Chris and Joe assured me that I could handle the hot temperatures with my running experience and new hydration strategies.

After arriving at home, I reflected on our conversation for the next few days and then viewed the Sulphur Springs website. I searched for the 100-kilometre distance for a while but I couldn't find it—the race directors had gotten rid of it. I reasoned that I would sign up for the 100-mile distance and only run 100 kilometres, and I sent Chris a text message to let him know.

"You're going to sign up for the 100 miler and run the 100 miler," was Chris's response.

Ultraliving Lessons

Temporary Setbacks

My sister Jacquie, mom, and dad heard a motivational speech from David "Tuffy" Knight when Jacquie was in high school and training at a high level for figure skating. Tuffy was the coach of the Wilfrid Laurier University football team in Waterloo, Ontario at the time. He was an exceptional coach and retired with 153 wins, setting the record for the most wins in Canadian university football history. Tuffy was a fiery speaker and although I didn't hear his talk personally, my dad would recount Tuffy's speech to me throughout my teenage years. Tuffy's main message was to view defeats as temporary setbacks. Losing is tough and it can make you feel terrible, but losing will not keep you down permanently. The most important thing that you can do is to recognize a defeat as a temporary setback. You don't need to give up on your goal because of that defeat. You can view the loss as a learning experience and then go back with ferocity as you attack your goal.

It took me a while to realize that I had learned some valuable lessons at Sulphur Springs. I learned the critical importance of hydration and nutrition planning and to act quickly to remedy dehydration. Although it took some time, I began to view Sulphur Springs as a temporary setback.

Sulphur Springs 100 Miler - May 2018

"Have you signed up for Sulphur Springs yet?" Joe asked.

I sheepishly admitted that I had not. Joe and I were chatting in front of a vegetable stand in downtown Georgetown. The sun shone and it was a particularly warm day for early October. My family and I were visiting the local farmers market on a Saturday when we ran into Joe. Joe encouraged me to sign up for Sulphur Springs that same day and I knew what he was getting at. He wanted me to take advantage of my motivation while I had it.

We enjoyed a nice lunch as a family after we got back home from the market. Distracted from my conversation with Joe, I stepped away to my home office after lunch and I logged on to the Sulphur Springs website. Was I really going to do this? I moved the cursor over to the 100-mile race option, held my breath, and clicked the button. I was going back to Sulphur Springs and this time I was going to attempt 100 miles.

I had over six months to prepare for Sulphur Springs since the race was at the end of May. Over the next few weeks I got to work building a training plan. One of my biggest challenges was finding the time to train around the demands of my family. A lot of people use a busy family life as an excuse for skipping training, but I firmly believe that you can complete your goals if you are strategic with your time. I planned most of my runs so that I would minimize the amount of time away from my family. I chose to run at lunch during the week while the kids were at school and early in the mornings on weekends while my family was asleep.

The weeks went by as I built up my running mileage. Sulphur Springs was now only 10 weeks away and my training was going great, until I hit my head on James's bunk bed. I was tucking James in one night after a long training session earlier in the day. James sleeps on the bottom bunk and I was so tired that I forgot to duck my head to avoid hitting the top bunk after giving James a hug goodnight. I was worried that I had a concussion but was hopeful that I could sleep it off. To my dismay, I woke up the next day and felt the familiar brain fog. I toned down my training for the next week and monitored how I was feeling. Fortunately, my concussion symptoms improved and I resumed a modified training plan.

I slowly got back on track with my running as the concussion symptoms subsided. Sulphur Springs was only four weeks away when I ran into more problems. I was halfway through a long trail run when I hit my head on a low hanging branch. It wasn't one of my brightest moments; I didn't see the branch because I was looking at my phone. I woke up the next day with brain fog and a sense of panic. I had my longest training runs coming up and I didn't know how I was going to finish them with concussion symptoms.

I lightened my training once more for a week but my symptoms didn't improve this time. I began to feel very anxious about the race. Anxiety and depression are among the post-concussion syndrome symptoms and I had experienced some significant anxiety from concussions in the past. I tend to perseverate on my symptoms when I've had a concussion, by actively thinking about how I'm feeling every few minutes. I wondered if my symptoms were only imagined and if I was subconsciously trying to get out of the race.

Sulphur Springs was now three weeks away and I had back-to-back four-hour training runs scheduled for Saturday and Sunday. I discussed my situation with Chris early in the week at Norah's swim practice. Norah and James had both joined the swim club that year with Chris as their head coach. Having coached swimmers for so long, Chris was used to dealing with athletes in crisis. He listened to my concerns about running with a concussion and suggested that I attempt the long runs and see how I felt. Chris even offered to do the Saturday long run with me and I gladly accepted.

Chris and I started our training session mid-morning on Saturday. We ran on the Bruce Trail at the Silver Creek Conservation area, a 15-minute drive north of Georgetown. The sun shone brightly in a cloudless blue sky. Birds chirped as we took in the vistas over Silver Creek, meandering trails that passed moss-covered, rocky outcroppings. Now in May, the forest still had remnants of snow cover. Spring was breaking through after a long winter and the sights and sounds of the trail were a great distraction from my concussion concerns. Chris and I ran for the full four hours together and I felt great after the session. My PCS symptoms had not worsened and I kept a good pace for the duration of the run. Having my confidence back, I completed Sunday's training session by myself. I finished the weekend feeling grateful for Chris's encouragement, which helped me get past my anxiety. Concussions are very serious and should be dealt with accordingly; however, I knew that anxiety had gotten the best of me in this situation.

I kept a close eye on the weather in the weeks leading up to the race. Despite my wish for something different, the forecast kept indicating hot weather for Sulphur Springs. Now, three days before the race, I accepted the hard truth of the forecast—it was going to be a hot and humid 34°C, the same temperature as the last time I ran Sulphur Springs. But I wasn't going to let the heat defeat me this time. I had written out a heat strategy in the few weeks leading up to Sulphur Springs. I planned to take at least one salt pill every half hour without fail. I would carry two 500 millilitre water flasks in the front of my hydration vest and a one-litre bladder in the back. To ensure that I stayed hydrated, I would drink one litre of water every time I completed a 20-kilometre lap. I would also wear my wide-brimmed Tilley hat that I wore during my hiking trip in Chamonix. Finally, I planned on running hard in the morning when it was cool, slowing down in the afternoon when it got hot, and then speeding up again when the sun went down.

Two anticipation-filled days went by before I woke up on the Friday morning feeling nervous but determined. I took the whole day off work, having learned my lesson from last time. I wanted to be fully rested before my run and I knew that working the whole day on Friday would make me feel tired on Saturday. Chris and I got to the start/finish area just after lunch and set up Joe's large tent. Set-up didn't take very long and we had the rest of the day to lounge around in lawn chairs, listening to music, eating chips, and drinking water.

Chris and I went to the 100-mile dinner and race briefi[ng]
day. The race staff had arranged for a food truck and Chris
few other runners and chatted as we ate. The race director (R
runners after most of us were finished our meals. In his mi
donned a Sulphur Springs T-shirt and loose-fitting jogging
with a big smile on his face as he explained the course. The Sulphur Springs 100 Miler was made up of eight 20-kilometre loops with hilly sections. There was one particularly hilly section halfway through the loop called The Three Sisters, named for three back-to-back hills with a total of nearly 300 metres in elevation. The RD also stressed the 30-hour cut-off time and he ended his talk by addressing the topic that was at the forefront of my mind—the weather.

"It's going to be stinking hot. Be prepared for it. It was stinking hot two years ago and we had the most 100-mile finishers ever. The reason for this is that racers slowed down."

Chris and I looked at each other and nodded. The RD had just predicted with certainty that it was going to be hot like the year I ran the 50-kilometre race and peed blood. For some reason, that declaration took away a lot of my anxiety about the weather. I didn't have to guess anymore about the weather. I knew it was going to be extremely hot and I was going to have to deal with it.

I woke up the next day to the sound of a gasoline-powered generator. Our tent was located 50 metres from the start line and we could hear the staff preparing for the race. I checked my watch and it was 4:30 a.m., time to take a salt pill with some water. I proceeded to get dressed, eat breakfast, and prepare my race gear. Similar to the last time, the 100-mile and 50-mile races were scheduled to start at 6:00 a.m.

Chris and Joe accompanied me on my short walk to the start line. Joe had joined us later in the evening the previous day. After saying goodbye to my friends, I lined up mid-pack and felt a slew of emotions—nervous energy, excitement, and pride. I was glad to be among these racers instead of being a spectator like two years before. The RD counted down from 10 and the race started with some cheers from the small crowd. Chris and Joe had stayed to see me off and cheered while I ran past. Starting this race felt surreal; I had gone through a lot to get here. I knew that my first 100-mile race would be a special experience and I did my best to take it all in.

...shed the first 20-kilometre loop without much trouble in a time of ...rs, 37 minutes. The weather was cool and I still felt the excitement from ...e start line. I completed another loop and checked my time as I ran into base camp. That loop had taken me a bit longer, 2 hours, 46 minutes. Chris had prepared two full 500 millilitre water bottles for me and I gulped them down. True to form at Sulphur, the temperature had risen to a steamy 34°C.

Determined to follow my plan for the heat, I left base camp for loop 3 wearing my wide-brimmed Tilley hat and running at a slower pace. Feeling okay, I arrived at the first aid station after an hour of running. I filled up my water bottles, ate a few chips, and put a handful of ice under my hat. The weather wasn't all bad, as clouds moved in and blocked the sun's full force shortly after I left the aid station. Making my way through the heat and humidity, I kept moving and arrived back at base camp a little before 3:00 p.m. I definitely felt the heat and I finished the loop in 3 hours, 30 minutes, 45 minutes slower than my previous loop. I was almost through the hottest part of the day, though, if I could just hang on until the evening. I drank my two bottles of water, chatted briefly with Chris and Joe, and then left on loop 4.

I plodded on through the heat. The air was sticky with humidity and all my clothes, from my shoes to my hat, were soaked with sweat. I had been on the course for over 10 hours at that point and I went into autopilot, running without thinking. It wasn't until I came across another 100-mile runner that I took some time to reflect on my condition. I asked the runner how he was doing as I ran past him. He was around my age and looked like a strong runner. He was walking through a particularly hot stretch of trail, as there wasn't any shade from the intense sun. He said that he was feeling dizzy so he decided to walk for a while. I told him that was a good idea and wished him luck as I continued to run.

As I ran on, I quickly realized that I was also feeling dizzy. That brief interaction had snapped me out of autopilot and I stopped to wait for a couple of minutes so I could walk with the runner I had just passed. I learned that he was in second place overall at one point until he started to feel the effects of the heat. I paced with that runner for around 20 minutes and then wished him luck again as I started to run. Fortunately, my dizziness went away and I managed a slow run for the remaining two hours it took me to complete the loop. With a big smile on my face, I ran into base camp at 6:30 p.m. I had made it through the hottest part of the day. Sure, I had more than 12 hours of running left, but I was looking forward to running in the cool night weather.

I left on loop 5 basking in the cooler temperature. Although I felt better, I didn't run any faster. I finished the loop without any incident; however, it was my slowest loop yet at 3 hours, 46 minutes. I was feeling down about my time until I saw Lindsay, the kids, and my in-laws waiting for me at the finish area. They cheered as I came through and I greeted my kids with big, sweaty hugs. Joe was waiting for me as well and he joined me as a pacer for loop 6. I was looking forward to having the company after being alone on the trail for most of the day. I burned more time than usual at base camp, enjoying the time with my family, and I got some stern looks from Chris as the minutes ticked away. It was time to get back on the course. I had a job to do.

Joe and I left base camp a little before 10:00 p.m. with our headlamps turned on. I was moving slowly and Joe got way out in front. Joe wanted to do a slow run but he ended up doing a fast hike and I still couldn't keep up. Despite moving slowly, we were having a nice time running at night. We almost had a full moon and I enjoyed the calm and the silence of the woods. We were about halfway through the loop when Joe asked me if I had eaten any solid food. I told Joe that I was taking gels but that I couldn't handle any solid food.

We got to the last aid station before base camp and Joe decided to intervene.

"What's the highest calorie food that you have here?" Joe asked the volunteer at the aid station.

"Well, we have butter tarts," said the volunteer.

Joe picked up three butter tarts and handed them to me.

"Here, eat these."

I reluctantly took the butter tarts and carried them with me for the five kilometres back to base camp. That loop had taken 4 hours, my slowest one yet. Chris and Joe had a private conversation while I filled up my water at our tent, and I joined them when I was ready to go back out.

"You're really slowing down. You need to eat some real food," said Joe.

"You've got to eat those butter tarts now," said Chris.

I took one bite of a butter tart and it coated my mouth like sawdust. Two sips of water helped transform the bite into a gooey mash so I could finally swallow it. I repeated the process until I had finally eaten two butter tarts.

They sat like bricks in my stomach and were accompanied by a wave of intense nausea. I doubled over with hands on my knees; I was going to throw up. Fortunately, the intensity of the nausea subsided after a few minutes and I avoided vomiting. My stomach still ached when we decided that I was less likely to throw up if I started moving again. Chris was pacing me for loop 7 and we left base camp a little after 2:00 a.m.

We were stopped by the RD as we were about to get back on the course. He had been monitoring my time and was concerned that I wouldn't make the 30-hour cut-off if I continued slowing down. I had 10 hours left to complete my last two loops.

"There's a 60-year-old lady who's beating you," said the RD.

I knew that he was trying to motivate me but he ended up just making me feel bad. I started my second last loop discouraged and feeling like I was going to puke.

Chris and I had been running for about five minutes when I noticed a small spring in my step. I tested a slightly faster pace for the next 15 minutes and was delighted that I could hold it. Miraculously, my stomachache subsided and I picked up the pace. Chris and Joe were on to something with those butter tarts. We got to the next aid station an hour later and a volunteer asked me what I wanted.

"Do you have any butter tarts?" I asked.

Chris's jaw dropped. Unfortunately, the aid station was out of butter tarts, so I opted for a good helping of peanut butter and jam sandwiches. Eating came with the familiar bout of intense nausea; however, I did my best to ignore it since I knew the feeling was temporary. Sure enough, I got over the nausea in about 15 minutes and continued to feel better. I finished loop 7 in a strong 3 hours, 42 minutes, 18 minutes faster than my previous loop.

Joe joined me for my final loop and we left base camp at around 7:00 a.m. The 30-hour cut-off time was on my mind. We had six hours left to finish, which seemed like enough time, though anything can happen in a 100-mile race.

The miles ticked by as Joe and I made our way around the course.

"You have nine miles left."

"Now it's six miles."

I couldn't believe that I was into single digits for remaining miles. My legs screamed as we climbed and descended the hilly sections of the course. We passed a young mom with her two kids out for a morning hike and the mom asked how long we had been running for.

"Ninety-eight miles," Joe responded.

Looks of disbelief flashed across the faces of the family.

We finally made it to the last climb and to the finish line. I exchanged a high five with Joe and then he stepped off the course as we got closer to base camp. I could see Lindsay and the kids waiting for me at the finish line, cheering me on. My eight year old, Norah, ran out to join me and we crossed the finish line together, our hands joined and held high in the air. Barely holding back tears, I was overcome with emotion—extreme joy, pride, and relief. The RD gave my finisher's medal to Norah and I wiped a tear from my eye as Norah slid the medal over my neck. James and David came to stand with me while the RD presented me with my first 100-mile belt buckle, and I gladly accepted the gleaming piece of hardware. Chris and Joe greeted me at base camp with hugs and handshakes. Although I had done most of the running on my own, finishing the race was certainly a team effort and I was so appreciative of their help. My final time was 27 hours, 38 minutes—23rd place out of 66 runners. More importantly, I had beaten the heat, the obstacle that I had built up so much in my mind.

Ultraliving Lessons

Creative Problem Solving

Ultrarunner Lucy Bartholomew refers to racing ultramarathons as "eating and problem solving with some running in-between" (Bartholomew 2019). A newcomer to the sport, Bartholomew surprised everyone by placing third female overall at the 2018 Western States 100-Mile Endurance Run (Western States). What was even more impressive . . . it was her first 100-mile race. Western States is considered the ultrarunning championship in North America and it takes place annually in Auburn, California at the end of June.

Bartholomew's description of ultrarunning is very accurate: a successful race is closely correlated to eating and solving the inevitable problems that come up. Although the butter tarts almost made me throw up, they were exactly what I needed at that point in the Sulphur Springs 100 Miler. Joe showed some great creativity by finding the highest calorie food to get me past my energy low. Creativity with gear was also critical since wearing my Tilley hat was very helpful for dealing with the heat.

Creative problem solving has helped me with other facets of life as well. I've made it past some significant life obstacles with short brainstorming sessions. I'll take 15 minutes to journal in the morning, jotting down ideas. Later in the day, I'll share these ideas with Lindsay or a friend. I've been amazed how someone else's perspective can help. Lindsay helps me validate my thinking or points me in the right direction if I'm going down the wrong path. When I come across a seemingly immovable obstacle in my life, I remind myself of the butter tarts. The solution to my racing problems at Sulphur was waiting for me at the aid station.

The Power of a Smile

I made a conscious effort to smile frequently during the Sulphur Springs 100 Miler. Aid stations were set up at every 10 kilometres along the course and I made sure to smile at the volunteers during every aid station stop. Smiling was the last thing that I felt like doing, but I smiled anyway. The aid-station volunteers had big smiles for me in return and told me how fresh I looked. Smiling helped me believe that I was actually doing okay. A 2018 article in *Runner's World* cites scientific evidence that smiling actually makes you run faster (Runner's World 2018). The researchers believed that smiling helps runners relax and have less muscle tension (Brick, McElhinney, and Metcalfe 2018).

I also decided that I would never complain about how I felt during Sulphur. I was often asked, "How are you doing?" by volunteers, family, and friends. I felt terrible later in the race; however, I never let on that I was struggling. Running 100 miles is a massive effort and I needed to carefully control my thoughts and emotions to ensure that I finished. Letting the smallest amount of negative emotion come through during an ultramarathon has the potential to lead to dark places which could lead to dropping out of the race.

Squamish Running Weekend - June 2018

Chris couldn't go any farther; his feet were freezing even though it was the end of June. Sitting on the ground, Chris, Joe, and I took in our surroundings. The snow, fog, and lack of trees had a disorienting effect. We thought that we were close to the summit of Black Tusk Mountain but we couldn't be sure.

"Does anyone have an extra pair of socks, by any chance?" Chris asked.

Chris went on to explain that he had holes in his shoes that were letting the snow in. As he's not one to stop our progress on the trails, I knew that Chris's feet must be in bad shape. I certainly didn't have an extra pair; I usually only pack socks for a longer race. Joe surprised us by miraculously producing a pair of wool socks from his pack. He didn't even realize he was carrying them. Chris gladly swapped his wet socks for the dry ones and got to his feet.

With that problem solved, we tackled our next issue, which was summiting Black Tusk in the fog. After a healthy debate, we decided to turn around and follow our tracks back down the mountain. Although we were all in great shape for running, none of us had experience in the mountains. We had just arrived in British Columbia and didn't want to begin our trip by getting lost.

Fortunately, the fog dissipated as we descended Black Tusk. Feeling more comfortable, we picked up the pace, having fun in the snow. We had seen videos of professionals running in the snow and it always looked like a blast. Mimicking the pros, we ran fast, while slipping, sliding, and jumping. We made it out of the snow and continued downhill. I kept expecting the trails to flatten out but our descent seemed endless. At 2,319 metres in elevation, Black Tusk was very different from the 200-metre hills in Georgetown that we were used to. Chris and Joe took off, running fast and whooping as they descended. I had a hard time keeping up, but I was having fun running on my own. My legs felt weaker than usual because of the 100 miler that I had run the month before. We arrived back at the parking lot after more than an hour of downhill running. With big smiles and high fives, we headed back to our Airbnb rental. We had another two days of running ahead of us.

Chris, Joe, and I had planned our running trip in April, a month before the Sulphur Springs 100 Miler. I needed to travel to Vancouver for business at the end of June and asked Chris and Joe if they wanted to make a running trip out of it. We settled on visiting Squamish, since it's considered the outdoor capital of Canada. Gary Robbins, one of our favourite professional ultrarunners, lived in North Vancouver at the time and we knew that he spent a lot of time in Squamish. Although it was a long shot, we hoped that we might cross paths with Gary Robbins in Squamish.

We got up at around 7:00 a.m. the day after our Black Tusk run and I told Chris and Joe that I was going to make a coffee run to Starbucks.

"There's no way we're going to Starbucks," said Chris with a smile.

Chris wanted to support the local businesses and had read about the Zephyr Café located in downtown Squamish. We drove together to the Zephyr Café and it didn't disappoint. Zephyr had a rustic vibe, with paintings by local artists on the wall and live edge bar tables near the wall-to-wall windows at the store front. Chris, Joe, and I discussed our plans for the day as we sipped coffee and ate vegan muffins. We settled on running the course for the Squamish 50, a local trail race directed by Gary Robbins. Taking place on a weekend in late August, the Squamish 50 has two distances: a 50 miler on the Saturday and a 50 kilometre on the Sunday. Ambitious runners will complete the 50/50, running both races.

Halfway through our breakfast, three people walked in who looked like trail runners: two ladies in their thirties and a man in his mid-forties, all wearing trucker hats and trail shoes. I mentioned to Chris and Joe that we should ask them about Squamish 50. We didn't feel confident navigating the course, even though we had brought maps with us. Feeling shy, we decided it was a long shot that these three would know the Squamish 50 course and decided not to approach them.

As we were about to leave, I decided to take a chance and chat with the trail runners. I walked over to their table and asked if they knew about Squamish 50. I was surprised by their reaction. One of the ladies explained that they were on their way to do a group training run for the race. They were going to finish their breakfast and then head over to a local sporting store to meet with the race directors of Squamish 50. She invited us along, but told me that we needed to hurry because the run started in less than an hour. Chris, Joe, and I made a split decision to hustle back to our place to change so that we could do the training run.

We pulled into the parking lot of Escape Route, a large sporting store near the north side of Squamish. A group of 15 runners made a line out the door. We wiggled our way into the store and found that it was standing room only. The race briefing had been underway when we arrived. A familiar voice gave the briefing; however, it was so crowded that I couldn't see who it was. I stood up on my tiptoes and caught a glimpse of one of none other than Gary Robbins.

Gary Robbins is the star of the movie *Where Dreams Go to Die*, a documentary about Gary's 2017 and 2018 attempts of the Barkley Marathons. The Barkley Marathons is considered one of the toughest races in the world, a 100 miler in Frozen Head State Park near Wartburg, Tennessee that consists of five laps of a 20-mile loop. Unlike other 100 milers, the Barkley course is unmarked and runners have to navigate their way around the course using maps and compasses. Only 15 runners have ever completed the race since its inception in 1995. Chris, Joe, and I had all watched this movie and had been seriously moved by Gary's efforts at Barkley.

Gary finished the briefing by asking everyone to ensure their names and cellphone numbers were on their participant list and he directed runners to a volunteer holding a clipboard. We didn't feel great about it, but Chris, Joe, and I reluctantly agreed that we would avoid signing the participant list. We thought the training run was only for official participants of the actual

Squamish 50 and we didn't want to miss an opportunity to participate in the training run.

As we waited outside Escape Route, I looked around at the 120 other runners and couldn't believe our luck. Less than an hour ago, we were sitting in a cafe figuring out what to do and now we were running an unofficial trail race directed by Gary Robbins. A volunteer started the race and we were off, running down a residential street. The road running continued for 10 minutes until we hit the trails. While Black Tusk was manicured and open, these trails were rugged with dense, green forest. We made our way past giant ferns and tall trees.

Chatting with other runners as we went, we exchanged stories of trail races from different parts of Canada. Most of the runners were from British Columbia and we enjoyed hearing about their local races. We had covered 10 kilometres when we caught up to two ladies who looked like they were in their late thirties. They were both moving well over the technical terrain and it was clear that they were experienced trail runners. One of the ladies was very outgoing and she shared that she had run the Grouse Grind for 24 hours the previous weekend to raise money for cancer. On Grouse Mountain in North Vancouver, the Grind is a 2.9-kilometre climb with 853 metres of elevation and 2,830 stairs. I was impressed that she was moving so well after such a big effort. She also shared that she was not running the official Squamish 50 race this year. I was relieved to hear this and I let it slip that we didn't sign up for the training run. She glanced at me sideways and told me that we should have registered, as it was important for the race staff to keep track of us on the mountains. She mentioned that we could register at the halfway aid station and that we should pay the five dollars to cover the food that was provided. Embarrassed, I agreed that we would sign up when we reached the aid station.

Chris, Joe, and I were all in good spirits when we arrived at the aid station after running roughly 17 kilometres. We had encountered some challenging climbs; however, we handled them without much difficulty. We found the race volunteer with the clipboard and sheepishly explained that we forgot to sign up at the beginning of the race. With a polite smile, the race volunteer collected our money and asked us to choose our distance: 35 kilometres or 50 kilometres. Joe and I pushed for the 50-kilometre course but Chris was skeptical. He thought that we hadn't seen the most challenging part of the course yet and urged that we play it safe. Joe and I reluctantly agreed to do the

35-kilometre course even though I thought it was going to be easy. We filled up our water, ate some chips, and then got back on our way.

The terrain became challenging almost immediately after we left the aid station and we climbed two good-sized mountains in the next hour. Our progress slowed due to the climbs and we were passed by two local runners who warned us that we had more climbing ahead of us. With this foreshadowing, we began to climb a trail called Galactic Scheisse, which is German for "Galactic Shit." The trail didn't betray its name and it climbed over 400 metres in 2.7 kilometres. Halfway up Galactic Scheisse, I bonked and my legs cramped badly. I went into emergency mode and took four salt pills and ate two energy gels. Chris and Joe laughed when they saw me taking the excessive amount of salt. I was already taking at least two salt pills every half hour. This must have been what I needed, though, because my cramps dissipated and I slowly gained back energy as we continued the tough climb.

We heard a shrill scream as we neared the top of Galactic Scheisse. Ten minutes went by and I almost screamed as a large grouse surprised us only a few feet off the trail. Protecting its nest, the grouse gobbled loudly and showed an aggressive posture. Clearly, the grouse wanted us to go away.

We finally summited the mountain and started on the last 10 kilometres. I had run out of water at that point and Chris offered me a drink since he had a full 500 millilitre water bottle left. I promptly drank the whole bottle.

"Thanks buddy, I really needed that!" I said.

"You drank the whole thing? I meant that you could have a sip," said Chris.

We came off the trails and onto dirt roads for the final few kilometres of the run. Moving slowly and feeling tired, Joe and I admitted that Chris had been right—we were all glad that we had chosen to do the 35-kilometre course. Now on the last kilometre, we got on to residential streets and picked up our pace, excited at the prospect of meeting Gary Robbins. I questioned Chris and Joe about asking Gary to take a photo with us, being mindful that this might sound cheesy.

"I was totally planning on taking a picture with Gary," said Chris.

With that decided on, we ran hard and saw Gary sitting at the finish line back where we started at Escape Route. Gary stood up and shook hands with us as we crossed the finish line. He took a good five minutes to chat and he was impressed that we had flown from Ontario to do his training run. We followed through on our plan and took a group picture with Gary, which we promptly posted to Instagram. Later that day, Gary even gave us a nice comment on our Instagram photo.

We spent our final day in Squamish climbing the iconic Stawamus Chief. The Chief is one of the largest boulders in the world, at a towering 702 metres of elevation. A popular tourist destination, the trail up the mountain is well marked with stairs and banisters. This run was far less rugged than our previous ones but it was still challenging. We got to the Chief at around 10:00 a.m. and it didn't take us long to reach the top. On that beautiful sunny day, we were blown away by the amazing views. We took in the panorama—the sparkling blue ocean, rivers, mountains, and forests.

We climbed down the Chief and then headed back to our Airbnb. It was Sunday afternoon and we needed to leave for Vancouver so Chris and Joe could catch a flight back to Toronto and I could start work the next day. Leaving Squamish was bittersweet. We were sad to leave such a beautiful place, yet we had made some amazing memories.

It would be a while before I got to test myself on the trails again. I had been promoted to national sales manager at work and was expected to travel around Canada for the next few months. Since I would be travelling during the week, I didn't want to spend weekends racing and away from my family. I was in a groove with running but I had a bumpy road ahead of me. Stress from my new job was about to bring out some demons from my past.

Ultraliving Lessons

Proximity

The Law of Success by Napoleon Hill is a famous business book which was first published in 1928. In the book, Napoleon Hill shares an impactful lesson about getting as close as you can to your goals. Hill tells the story of Edwin C. Barnes, a man who was determined to become business partners with Thomas Edison, the inventor of the light bulb and the Elon Musk of his day. Barnes couldn't afford a train ticket so he hopped a freight train to Edison's laboratory in New Jersey. Barnes wanted to be as close as possible to the inventor and took a job as the laboratory's janitor. It took Barnes a few years but he would eventually reach his goal of becoming Edison's business partner.

Barnes would become wealthy and successful, primarily because of his proximity to Edison.

Chris, Joe, and I really wanted to meet Gary Robbins but we knew it was a long shot. We decided to try anyway and got as close as possible to the trails that Gary runs. We had no idea how we were going to meet Gary, but we caught a lucky break because of our proximity to him.

This lesson can be applied to life goals as well. An actor who dreams of making it big should consider moving to Hollywood. Being close to all the action is sure to help an actor's chances of getting that first big role. On a smaller scale, a great way to start trail running is to get close with other trail runners. I've benefited immensely from my friendship with Chris over the years. I have learned valuable lessons about trail running that would have taken me years to learn on my own. I continue to learn from the online relationships that I have developed as well. Becoming friends with other trail runners on Instagram, or joining Facebook groups, is a great way to get more involved in trail running. I've learned about local races, fastest known times, and tips and tricks, all through social media.

Horror Trail Race - October 2018

The scale in my bathroom read 215 pounds. Certain it must not be working properly, I stepped off the scale so that it could reset and then I got back on. It read 215 pounds again. I had a trail race coming up in a month, which wasn't enough time to lose the 15 pounds I had gained since the Squamish running trip. My new job was the culprit; the added responsibility was stressful and I had packed on the pounds as a result. I had also signed up for the Horror Trail Race, a six-hour ultramarathon that took place outside of Kitchener, Ontario right before Halloween. I decided to compartmentalize my negative feelings and continue moving forward. I was going to do my best with my current situation.

A few months prior to the Horror Trail Race, I made a goal to come in the top 10 finishers of the race. I pulled the online results from the previous year and noticed that the top five finishers had run around 55 kilometres in six hours. The race course is 2.5 kilometres and runners complete as many loops as possible in six hours. I designed my training plan so that I could build up to running 30 kilometres in three hours. I didn't want to spend more than three hours on my training runs, to limit the time away from my family. Business travel was already keeping me away one to two weeks per month.

Despite tipping the scales at 215 pounds, my training progressed well. Two weeks before the race, I listened to a timely podcast interview with professional ultrarunner Karl Meltzer. I really like Meltzer's racing philosophy, which is summed up by his catch phrase "100 miles isn't that far." During the interview, Meltzer talked about different strategies for racing and compared the benefits of keeping a predetermined pace vs. going out fast and seeing if you could hold on. Meltzer has run hundreds of 100-mile races and he holds the overall record for the most 100-mile wins in history. Out of all those races, Meltzer says that he has only had a few perfect races: days where he feels amazing and can run effortlessly. He urges that you should always put yourself in a position to take advantage of a perfect day. Start the race at an aggressive pace and pull back if needed; it's tough to do the opposite. If you start off at a slow pace and realize that you're feeling great, it's often too late to take advantage of a perfect-day feeling. Karl's racing strategy struck a chord and I decided to go out fast in the Horror Trail Race and see if I could hold on. The race was only six hours after all, nothing compared to a 100 miler.

On race day, I woke up early and drove for an hour to the race site, Camp Heidelberg, which is an outdoor education centre on 73 acres of woods just outside of Kitchener, Ontario. I picked up my bib from the registration table inside the centrally located two-story building on the property. Since the start time was an hour away, I set up my own little aid station beside the building. I had brought a plastic bin with racing food and gear. I had half an hour to burn before the race started, so I explored some of the course. The 2.5-kilometre loop started in an open field near the main building and after 300 metres the course passed a large pavilion with an aid station. Signs then directed runners to a trail that travelled into the woods. The trail eventually looped back towards the highway that I had driven in on. I knew that it was going to be tough to run the same loop for six hours, but at least there was some variety in scenery.

Now with only five minutes left before the race, I made my way to the front of the pack of runners, right behind the start line. The race director counted down from 10 and then I was off, running fast as planned. My pace felt good as I discovered the course on my first lap—a nice pond after the aid station, a fairly steep hill that was already slick with mud, and winding single track as I got deeper into the forested area. I finished my first lap in the top five. Running fast continued to feel good and I held pace for the first

10 kilometres, clocking in at 53 minutes and staying in the top five. I made a quick stop at my bin of supplies to take a gel and a salt pill, something I planned on doing every hour.

Registering more loops, I ran on and completed another 10 kilometres in 57 minutes. So far, so good. Finishing another four loops in 54 minutes, I had now completed 30 kilometres. I held on to fifth place as I left for my 13th loop. While the earlier loops felt easy, I could now feel the strain of maintaining my aggressive pace for over three hours. I tried a new tactic and repeated a mantra in my head as I ran—cool, calm, confidence, and compete.

I had listened to a podcast interview with Rob Krar in the weeks leading up to the race. Born in Canada and now living in Flagstaff, Arizona, Krar is a well-known ultrarunner who is a two-time winner of the Western States Endurance Run 100 Miler. Krar mentioned that he repeats a mantra in his head while he races—composure, confidence, and compete (Yang, 2018). My adaptation of Krar's mantra helped me work through the pain and kept me focused during the race. It turned out to be a great tool.

I ran well for the next half hour, completing two more loops. I had completed three-quarters of another loop when I bonked hard and had to stop and walk. My quads cramped and seized as the sixth place runner passed me. I had never experienced a bonk like this before and I went into emergency mode and ran through a mental diagnostic. I had been drinking enough water and been taking salt pills and gels. I reasoned that I must need more food, as I hadn't eaten a meal in four hours and I had been getting all of my calories from gels. I walked and ran along the course, making slow progress until I got to my aid station. I devoured a Snickers bar along with two salt pills and felt better almost immediately. My bonk had taken its toll, though, and I finished my fourth 10 kilometres in 77 minutes, which was 23 minutes longer than my previous 10 kilometres.

Re-energized, I ran two more loops at a decent pace, completing a total of 45 kilometres. The energy didn't last, however, and I bonked again, slowing down to a walk for a good portion of a loop. I got back to my aid station and promptly ate another Snickers bar. Once again, the food helped me feel better. I ran another loop and finished a total of 50 kilometres.

It was getting close to the six-hour cut-off and I needed to push my pace if I wanted to break the top 10. At that point, I didn't know what place I was in, but I felt like I still had a good shot of completing my goal. Legs burning,

I ran past the familiar landmarks of the course. I passed the pavilion and then the pond, all the while glancing at my watch to ensure that I had enough time. I walked the muddy hill, navigating some parts on all fours since it was very slick by that point. I ran the single track through the woods, hoping that I could hold on to my pace until the finish line. Finally, I came out of the woods, through the open field, and then crossed the finish line. I had completed 52.5 kilometres with a few minutes to spare before the cut-off. For a split second, I considered stopping since I was so close to my car; however, I put those thoughts aside and continued running, almost sprinting, until I heard an air horn blast. I had squeezed in an extra kilometre for a total of 53.5 kilometres.

Since I completed a partial final loop, I needed to tell the timing official my distance. There was a lineup to see the official and I anxiously waited for my chance to speak with him. When it was finally my turn, the racing official tallied my results and told me that I had come in 11th place out of 25 runners. My heart sank since I had missed making the top 10 by one place. I didn't know how to feel about that result. Eleventh place was my best finish ever in an ultramarathon, but I didn't complete my goal of breaking the top 10.

Even more disappointing, I didn't believe that I actually finished in 11th place since my Garmin watch read only 51 kilometres. I decided to walk back to the timing official so that I could tell him I did one lap fewer than the official results. The timer assured me that I ran 53.5 kilometres and he said that the GPS signals for watches are often inaccurate on that course.

I don't know what it was about my mindset at that time. Perhaps it was burnout from the extremely busy September and October I had just experienced at work, but here is my journal entry from the day after the race:

> I ran the Horror Trail Run near St. Jacobs yesterday. For some reason I felt depressed about it after I finished the race. I ran 53.5 kilometres in six hours, which I thought was a pretty good result considering the shape I'm in. I haven't been doing any crazy long runs ... I had pretty high hopes leading up to the race and that must have been why I felt crappy about it when I finished. I'm also comparing myself to the top runners who are in very good shape. I probably weigh 40 pounds or more than the top guys. I know now that I need to lose around 10–15 pounds to get back to 200 pounds.

Clearly, I had to work through some baggage. I was happy with my effort during the race and the resourcefulness I had shown by recovering after bonking. But the race also revealed that I had an issue with my weight and it was a problem that I had been ignoring. Since it was a familiar challenge for me, I was upset that I had let it happen. I knew that I had work to do; however, it would take some time before I saw the results that I was looking for.

Ultraliving Lessons

Trust Your Toolkit

The Horror Trail Run was the first time I had run hard for six hours straight and I didn't know how my body would respond. As often happens in ultramarathons, I needed to improvise when I unexpectedly bonked later in the race. In my preparation for the race, I had reviewed my race reports and was reminded that I needed to eat something substantial when I hit a significant energy low. I was glad that I knew enough to go back to my toolkit when I bonked during the race. I had originally planned on only eating gels every 45 minutes during the race, but I brought chocolate bars just in case I needed more food.

I also packed extra gear, which played a critical role in helping me finish. I started the race wearing shorts and a long-sleeved shirt with a T-shirt over top. I was warm enough for the first few hours of the race until it started snowing at the 40-kilometre mark. I was freezing but I tried to push through the cold weather since I didn't want to waste time stopping. I was finally forced to stop when my arms became painful from the cold. I put on a rain jacket and gloves and felt better immediately. Without my extra gear, I might have needed to take a prolonged break to warm up inside the building. Whether it's a six-hour race or a 100-mile race, every experience holds valuable lessons. The more race reports that I create, the better the toolkit I have for my next race.

Sulphur Springs 50 km (Part 2) - May 2019

Running the Sulphur Springs 50 km was part of my new and ambitious plan. I went back to an old goal of mine—to run the UTMB. I was getting closer to my 40th birthday, having turned 37 earlier in the year. Lindsay and I decided that my 40th birthday was a great occasion for running the UTMB. I started researching the UTMB and learned about International Trail Running Association (ITRA) points. I would need to earn 15 ITRA points in a total of three races over the next two years to qualify for UTMB. Five ITRA points are given for completing a very difficult 100-kilometre race or a 100-mile race of regular difficulty. Six ITRA points are given for completing a very difficult 100-mile race. Unfortunately, I wasn't guaranteed entry to UTMB after earning the points since I would need to enter a draw with thousands of other runners. I decided to take my chances with the draw and get 15 points over the next two years. I would enter the UTMB draw in December 2020 so that I could race in August 2021, the year that I turned 40.

Finding a UTMB qualifying race in Canada isn't easy. When I searched for one in December 2018, there weren't any race options in my home province of Ontario. Race directors are required to pay an annual fee to ITRA and submit course information for the UTMB qualifier designation. Earning

ITRA points has caused a fair amount of controversy in the ultrarunning community. In an open letter to UTMB in June 2017, race directors for nine of the biggest trail races in the United States refused to pay for the ITRA designation. These race directors titled their letter "Why We Won't Pay: UTMB, ITRA and the 'Pay for Points' Racket." (Ultrarunning Magazine 2017).

I settled on running the Quebec Mega Trail (QMT) 110-kilometre race in June 2019 so that I could earn 5 ITRA points. I was excited about the course, which explored Mont-Sainte-Anne, one of the biggest ski hills in Quebec. I had fond memories of visiting Mont-Sainte-Anne for family ski trips as a child. With close to 5,000 metres of total elevation gain, I knew that QMT would be challenging. I added more weight training to my plan so that I would have enough strength for the big climbs. In addition to running, I incorporated one weight workout per week, which consisted of squats, deadlifts, ab crunches, and calf raises.

I signed up for the Sulphur Springs 50 km in February 2019. Sulphur took place at the end of May and I thought it would be a great training run for QMT. A lot of experienced ultrarunners recommend incorporating training races into your schedule to stay motivated.

I asked Chris and Joe if they wanted to race with me, but it didn't work out since all three of us were busy with our professional lives. Chris and I continued to train together, although I saw him less than I had the year before due to the demands of my new job. Joe had taken a break from ultrarunning so that he could focus on his schooling to become an osteopath.

I progressed well with my training through the winter months. While my running went well, the quality of my professional life deteriorated. I was working and traveling more than ever due to the demands of my job. I was away for almost two weeks of every month, working with my team on the road. It would have been easy to lay off on my running but I chose to stick with it. With the unrelenting work pressure, I had not lost any weight since the Horror Trail Race. I knew my weight was holding me back from better results in running, but I had too many balls in the air and felt like I didn't have room for any new priorities.

Winter turned to spring and it quickly became time to race the Sulphur 50 km. I felt giddy with anticipation the night before the race. Sure, I harboured negative feelings from my Sulphur experience in 2016; however, those feelings were overpowered by my positive experience with the 100 miler in 2018. I looked forward to getting back on the course that I had spent so much time on the previous year. I was so confident with my abilities in the heat that I only casually kept track of the anticipated weather for the race.

I got to Sulphur Springs early on race day and proudly wore my 100 mile-finisher sweatshirt. Watching the start of the 100-mile and 50-mile races, I noticed familiar faces of runners who had competed with me the year before. Shortly after, it started to rain and I sought shelter in my car. I reviewed my strategy in my mind since I had an hour to kill before the start of my race. Recognizing that this was a training race, I planned to run at an aggressive pace but not so fast that I would risk injury. The course was similar to the year before, with the same 20-kilometre loop that I had run so many times. For the 50-kilometre race, I would start with a modified 10-kilometre loop and then run the main 20-kilometre loop twice.

The rain stopped yet grey skies remained when it came time to line up for my race. Feeling ambitious, I went to the front of the pack and exchanged head nods and hellos with some serious looking runners. Three, two, one—the race started and we ran down the familiar big hill. The rain came back with a vengeance about 20 minutes in. Thunder cracks and lightning bolts raised eyebrows, though I continued to progress through the course. I'm okay with running in the rain but the lightning made me nervous. Despite the weather, I made good time and kept in the top 10 for my first 10-kilometre loop.

I continued to run aggressively as I left for my first 20-kilometre loop. Since I wasn't going to be on the course very long by ultrarunning standards, I decided to run straight through puddles rather than avoiding them. Halfway through this loop, I splashed through a particularly deep puddle, which was not appreciated by the two ladies who were taking great care to avoid the water. I yelled, "Sorry," as I splashed muddy water on their legs.

Completing my first 30 kilometres in good time, I got back on the course for my final loop. True to form for Sulphur, the sun burned away the rain clouds and the temperature rose above 30°C. A few kilometres in to the last loop, I realized that I hadn't peed in over two hours. I immediately took two salt pills and drank most of the water that I was carrying, planning to fill up my water at the next aid station. I knew better than to mess around with my hydration at Sulphur Springs.

Slipping and sliding on muddy terrain, I passed more timid runners who carefully found their footing on slick sections. I ran a little too fast on a muddy downhill about halfway through that loop and, losing my footing, I fell on to my back in warm mud and slid down the hill for a good 10 meters. I couldn't help laughing at myself when I finally came to a stop. I looked like I had emerged from a mud bath.

Continuing to make steady progress, I was now five kilometres from the finish line. I glanced behind me on a flat section of trail and noticed a 50-kilometre runner who was 100 metres behind me. Having run for five hours, I was tired but determined. I was not going to let this guy beat me. He came within 30 metres on the last large hill before the finish line. Mustering energy from an unknown reserve, I ran uphill with legs burning, trying my best to stay in front. Continuing to surprise myself, I broke into a near sprint for the last 50 metres of the hill. I ran through the finish line grimacing and grunting, and I'm sure I would have looked terrible if someone had taken my photo. Hands on my knees, I caught my breath while the runner behind me crossed the finish line.

"You're a beast!" he said.

While I liked my finisher's medal, I appreciated that compliment even more. That runner was in good shape and I could tell that he took running seriously. I finished in 5 hours, 28 minutes, 19th place out of 184 and with my best result ever at a 50-kilometre race.

Later that evening when I got home, I reviewed the post-race photo that I had taken and I was reminded that I still looked heavier than I should for optimal running. Oh well, I still had a strong showing. Besides, there wasn't much I could do about my weight at that point; I was running QMT in one month. Like before, I needed to push on and complete my training.

My strong result felt great, especially since that race was so challenging for me only a few years prior. I had gained some more valuable experience for my toolkit and bolstered my confidence. Pleased with my result, I concluded that I was in good enough shape for a solid showing at QMT. A few weeks later I would find out just how wrong I was.

Ultraliving Lesson

Continue Moving Forward

One of the great lessons from ultrarunning is that pain and discomfort are temporary. I've experienced painful low points in every ultramarathon that I've run. I have completed most of my races, though, since I've kept going by making steady progress through the low points.

Always continue moving forward, even when life gets really hard is a rule that I've developed since I've started running ultras. Similar to running an ultramarathon, you'll encounter extremely tough situations in your everyday life and it's important to continue making progress during those low points. My experience has shown me that circumstances often seem worse in your mind than they actually are. You might need to slow down and walk during a race, which feels discouraging. You feel like you are barely moving, when in reality you are making steady progress.

This mindset was very helpful during the time I trained for the Sulphur Springs 50 km. With work being so tough, I had somehow managed to keep a decent mindset, trusted that my situation would improve, and I moved forward in the best way that I could. Fortunately, I realized that nothing good would come from a negative mindset.

At work, when I have a tough meeting, I remind myself that I have been through much worse. If I lasted through an almost 28-hour ultramarathon, I can certainly last through an hour-long meeting. This mindset continues to help me deal with difficult people. I like to think that the person has another thing coming if they think they are going to get the best of me. They are dealing with an ultramarathoner.

Quebec Mega Trail 110 km - June 2019

I had made up my mind; I was going to drop out of the Quebec Mega Trail after having run 80 kilometres. When I shared that with Matt, he didn't try to convince me otherwise. Instead, Matt offered me a cheeseburger.

***

I sat down to make my race-day plan for Quebec Mega Trail (QMT) a week after Sulphur Springs. Since the Sulphur Springs 50 km took me 5 hours, 28 minutes, I figured that I could run the 110 kilometres of QMT in around 16 hours. Curiously, the QMT has a 24-hour cut-off, but I was sure that I would finish well before that.

I spent a few minutes each day visualizing the race in the last few weeks leading to the QMT. Ever since my days in university, I had used visualization to help prepare for big life events. I had studied the QMT course by reading about it on the web site and watching YouTube videos. Armed with my research, I wrote a detailed visualization, including how I would approach different sections of the course and how I would feel. All that visualization was done with the 16-hour time frame that I had estimated.

I flew to Montreal a week before the QMT. I had planned a business trip around the race and spent a few days working in the city before driving a rental car to Mont-Sainte-Anne, about four hours away.

My friend Matt met me in Mont-Sainte-Anne late on Thursday night. Similar to the way that I became friends with Chris, I had met Matt on the trails in Georgetown. We encountered each other a few times before we decided to meet up for a trail run. Continuing to meet for trail runs, Matt and I saw each other every month or two for the five years leading up to the QMT. On one of those trail runs, I mentioned to Matt that we were looking for a new house in Georgetown. Matt said that I should call his mom, Betty, who was a real estate agent, and it turned out that Betty was the agent selling the house we liked. Lindsay and I took that as a positive sign. We asked Betty to represent us and ultimately worked out a deal to buy our current home. Although Matt is around 10 years my junior, we get along really well, and I feel that Matt has an excellent grasp on life's priorities. Matt is an arborist and spends most of his days in the woods tending to trees. He has a friendly disposition, closely cropped dark hair and, a classic runner's build.

Matt and I spent the next day scoping out the area and getting ready for the race. In the morning we explored Beaupré, a small town neighbouring Mont-Sainte-Anne. After all the stress from my job, it was great to be a tourist for the day. We then drove to the race site in the afternoon to register and to walk around. I learned a few weeks earlier that the QMT was designated the Canadian ultrarunning championship for 2019. A large stage and a serious-looking finishing arch had been erected at the base of the mountain. To finish off the day, we had dinner at a brew pub on the St. Lawrence River called Microbrasserie des Beaux Prés. Sitting outside, drinking beer, and eating pizza, I soaked it all in. Matt took a phone call with Betty halfway through our meal and, to my surprise, Betty had picked up the tab for our meal.

We got to bed early on Friday night and before I knew it, it was 4:00 a.m. and time to wake up. Matt was going to meet me at the halfway aid station and then again at the 80-kilometre mark where he would pace me for the last 30 kilometres. I drove my rental car to the mountain and got on a bus that took me to the start line. In a light rain, we started off the race on a pier near Le Massif, one of the largest ski mountains in Quebec in a town called Petite-Rivière-Saint-François. The song "Xanadu" by Rush played over the PA system right before the start. The race director had mentioned this song in the online race briefing two weeks earlier. "Xanadu" had an awesome effect and the race started just as the song reached its crescendo. The crowd of runners surged with the music, crossing the starting arch and running onto the road. We ran on road through the town for about three kilometres and then started climbing into the mountains. The running was easy going and I reached the first aid station on the top of Le Massif without much difficulty.

I ran an easy 10 kilometres to the second aid station where I was greeted by a group of screaming volunteers. They were chanting "Joe, Joe, Joe" as I approached, and I realized that they were making up names for all the runners as they passed. Mildly amused, I left the aid station expecting more of the challenging yet manageable terrain. I couldn't have been more wrong.

I hit technical trails with sloppy mud, slippery rocks, and challenging climbs. To make matters worse, it was hot, but fortunately the shade in the woods kept the heat reasonable. Progress was painstakingly slow during the eight kilometres to the third aid station. When I arrived, I gave the campfire a wide berth—I didn't need any extra heat at that point. I was curious why the volunteers had started a fire until I had to start swatting mosquitoes. Apparently, I wasn't the only one who struggled with the conditions; I overheard three runners telling officials that they were dropping out. I was having a tough time but I wasn't ready to throw in the towel. Determined to keep going, I refilled my water, had some banana bread, and got back on the course.

The technical terrain continued as I descended for four kilometres, until, mercifully, I came out on a dirt road. I had been running for 500 metres when I met a runner in his mid-forties sitting on the back of an ATV. He explained that his knee wouldn't let him go any farther and that race officials were bringing him back to the base of Mont-Sainte-Anne. It was at that moment my first thoughts of dropping out crept in. I thought about how nice it would feel to get a ride back to my car. I quickly dismissed those thoughts, though, and pressed on. I was grateful to stretch my legs on the dirt road and to give my mind a break. I had done most of my training on only mildly technical terrain and the QMT's roots, rocks, and mud were taking their toll on me. I had to pay constant attention to every foot plant so that I didn't fall, which was physically and mentally exhausting. I was starting to doubt the feasibility of finishing in 16 hours; however, I wasn't ready to give up on my goal.

After a short stretch of easy running, I reached a water crossing that preceded the halfway aid station— Saint-Tite-des-Caps. I started wading through a 100-metre-long stretch of the river that ran under a bridge. About 20 metres ahead of me, a fellow runner named Jose fell and went completely underwater. Jose got up, found his footing, and then promptly went under again. I had been chatting with Jose half an hour earlier when he passed me on the dirt road. Determined not to go swimming, I picked a different route than Jose, hugging the side of the bridge's foundation. I successfully managed the water crossing, staying upright and dry.

I ran into the aid station and quickly found Matt. Planning for a 16-hour finish, I had asked Matt to meet me there over two hours earlier. I felt bad that Matt had been waiting for me so long but he didn't complain. He'd brought a camping chair and a book and had enjoyed the race's atmosphere. I sat down to change my socks in a pavilion that the race organizers had erected. Matt offered to make me a peanut butter, jam, and banana wrap and I gladly accepted. Matt had also brought me a change of clothes but I decided to continue on in my sweaty clothes, a decision I would later regret. Doing some mental math while chatting with Matt, I finally accepted that there was no way I was finishing the race in 16 hours. At the rate I was going, I'd finish in over 20 hours, a pace that would have us on the course past 2:00 a.m. I reluctantly asked Matt if he was okay with having a late night on the trails. Matt didn't miss a beat and said that he was definitely up for it. The interaction with Matt, the food, and the dry socks gave me a big morale boost and I got back on the trails feeling hopeful. I had completed 60 kilometres and had another 20 kilometres to get back to the Mont-Sainte-Anne aid station where Matt would be joining me as a pacer.

After running a short stretch of road, I turned back into the woods to start the Mestachibo section. My understanding is that Mestachibo means "Great River" in the Huron language and the name didn't disappoint. Fast-flowing blue water cut through a lush, green forest, with tall cliffs appearing sporadically. Despite its beauty, Mestachibo was a nightmare to navigate. The course ran alongside the rapids and went up and down a series of what seemed like never-ending small hills. The trail was slick with mud and packed with huge rocks and had several sections with ropes tied to trees to help with navigation. The Mestachibo section was only 10 kilometres long but I spent over two hours getting through it. When I finally emerged from the

Mestachibo section, I had made up my mind that I would drop out when I got to Mont-Sainte-Anne.

The sun was starting to set as I arrived at the Mont-Sainte-Anne aid station at 8:30 p.m. Matt greeted me with a big smile; however, I had a hard time holding eye contact—I wasn't proud of the decision I was about to share with him. Describing how tough the Mestachibo section was, I told Matt that I couldn't go on. Matt didn't show any disappointment and instead he asked if I wanted to sit down and have something to eat while we talked it over. I refused Matt's offer of a cheeseburger at first, but changed my mind after getting a few wafts of the delicious-smelling barbeque. Matt handed me the cheeseburger and I devoured it in a few bites. I had been eating gels and banana bread for the last five hours and it felt great to have something substantial in my stomach. As we talked, I began to reconsider my decision to drop. I shared with Matt that I could maybe go on if the rest of the course wasn't very technical. Matt asked a few of the volunteers about the remaining 30 kilometres and they assured him that the course was manageable, which is exactly what I needed to hear. I refilled my water and Matt and I set out to spend the night in the mountains.

* * *

My family and I had been to Mont-Sainte-Anne several times on ski vacations when I was growing up. With 71 different ski runs, Mont-Sainte-Anne offers a wide variety of challenging terrain. The most memorable ski run from my childhood was one called La Crête, which is a steep black diamond that seems almost vertical at some points. Being daredevils, my sister Jacquie and I loved schussing down La Crête. On a family ski trip in my early teens, Jacquie and I brought my dad to ski La Crête towards the end of our vacation. Jacquie and I skied at our regular aggressive speed and had to wait for dad at the bottom of the hill. When dad finally arrived, we asked him how he liked the run. Dad looked like he had seen a ghost. A solid skier, dad was conservative on the hill and generally avoided anything too aggressive. He shared that he feared for his life as he descended La Crête, which Jacquie and I thought was hilarious.

It must have been retributive justice for our earlier prank on dad. As Matt and I approached the mountain, we could see the course would lead us up a steep-looking ski run. The name of the slope came into focus as we continued to make progress. My heart dropped into my stomach when I realized it was La Crête.

I struggled to move at a good pace on our climb. My legs were extremely tired, and I had a nasty case of chafing between my legs since I had refused to change my clothes earlier in the race. There was nothing I could do about the chafing at that point, so I pushed on, ignoring the pain. Matt suggested that I use smaller steps to navigate the uphill. I tried the shorter stride and it worked well as we followed a mix of switchbacks and steep trail. We were greeted by a stunning view of Mont-Sainte-Anne as we neared the top of the mountain. The sun had almost set and a light fog shrouded the valley below. We paused to take in the sight and I reflected on how far I'd come. I would have missed this beautiful view had I dropped out of the race.

The sun had set completely by the time we covered the hard-fought 800 metres of elevation to the summit aid station. Hearing hoots and hollers as we neared, we could tell the aid station was staffed by a rowdy and good-natured group. Chatting at the aid station, the volunteers shared that we only had 21 kilometres left—12 kilometres to the next aid station and then nine kilometres to the finish. Matt led the way out of the aid station, setting a steady pace. Though very sore, I kept up with Matt as best as I could, running while leaning heavily on my trekking poles. The next 12 kilometres led us through winding trails. We travelled down ski runs, into the woods between slopes, and then would climb back up the mountain. Although challenging, that section was not nearly as technical as the earlier trails, as had been promised by the race staff. We made it to the final aid station and were greeted by a group of friendly but sleepy volunteers. Filling our water bottles for the last time, we were excited to make the last push to the finish. Matt continued to set an aggressive pace and we passed a few runners on a three-kilometre stretch of trail that led us to the base of the mountain.

Even though we only had three kilometres left, the QMT course had more surprises for us. We encountered a water crossing through a fast-flowing river. Matt wasn't keen on getting wet and somehow managed to hop from rock to rock, getting to the other side unscathed. I didn't have the energy for rock jumping and plowed through the river. The cold water felt good on my sore and blistered feet. Glad to have the water crossing behind us, we quickly encountered yet another water crossing. There were no boulders on that section and Matt resigned himself to getting wet. Moving away from the river, we could hear the music from the finish line, which helped us pick up the pace.

Rounding a bend, we could see the finisher's arch. I asked Matt to run through the finish line with me and we crossed the arch running side by side. After nearly giving up, I finished the QMT in 22 hours, 59 minutes, just before 5:00 a.m. Instead of receiving a medal, I was given a beautiful glass beer mug and told that I could fill it up in the chalet. I should have been thinking about breakfast, but a cold beer sounded amazing. I asked Matt if he wanted to have a beer and he nodded yes without hesitation. Both of us beer lovers, Matt and I had been talking about our post-race brews for a long time. I hobbled inside and sat down with Matt for a well-deserved celebratory beer.

After a few hours of sleep at our hotel, Matt and I parted ways. Matt drove back home and planned on making stops at one or two microbreweries. I returned my rental car at the Montreal airport and gingerly walked through the terminal to my gate. I had examined the chafing between my legs before leaving the hotel and cringed as I saw raised and red weeping wounds on my upper thighs. I highly regretted not changing my wet clothes as I walked like a saddle-sore cowboy onto the plane. Oh well, I hadn't done any permanent damage and I had a good new lesson for my toolkit.

Sitting on the plane, I took stock of the race. I had earned five hard-fought ITRA points and I was on my way to qualifying for UTMB. I was proud of my accomplishment and was so glad that I didn't drop out. I seemed to dwell on how I had wanted to give up though. Having followed my training plan closely, I knew that I had put in the work. The main reason for my lacklustre performance was present in the back of my mind and I was finally ready to deal with it. I had some serious work ahead of me to get ready for the 100-mile race that I had planned for the fall.

Ultraliving Lessons

Asking for Help

I had been hesitant to ask Matt to come with me. I don't like to burden or inconvenience anyone; it's the way I was raised. An ultrarunner himself, Matt was excited to join me and we ended up sharing a great experience, which has since strengthened our friendship.

Reflecting on my 100-mile race at Sulphur Springs, I had relied heavily on Chris and Joe to get me through the race. Ultrarunning might appear like a solitary sport, but it should be viewed as a team sport. Scott Jurek, who many consider the top trail runner of all time, had a support team for most of his big wins. Jurek's bestselling book *Eat and Run* describes his special relationship with Dusty Olson, a good friend who often paced and crewed for Jurek during big races.

I don't think I would have finished the QMT if Matt hadn't been there as my crew and pacer. In addition to Matt being extremely helpful, his presence gave me an extra level of accountability. Matt had driven close to ten hours to share that experience with me and I didn't want to let him down. I'm very grateful to have friends and family who support me with ultrarunning and I will continue to rely on them. Asking for help makes me feel uncomfortable at first; however, I know that it leads to amazing results.

Mental Preparation

I had a goal to finish the race in 16 hours and was very disappointed when I realized I couldn't achieve my goal. I was not mentally prepared for having to stay up all night and it was difficult to change my mindset during the race. Emotions can't always be trusted during an ultramarathon. A small problem can become a very big deal in your mind when you have been pushing yourself for hours on the trail. Emotions can be given a roadmap, though, through mental preparation.

I spend a lot of time visualizing before races. Writing in my journal, I make detailed descriptions of the course with the names of the different sections, the aid stations, the elevations, and the distances. I'll mentally rehearse how I would like the race to unfold, reading my journal several times before the race.

Making a big error, I had only visualized finishing the QMT in 16 hours. There was no plan B, no mental roadmap to fall back on, and I experienced a slew of negative emotions as a result. I'm sure that the negativity contributed to my wanting to drop out of the race. Taking careful note of that experience for my toolkit, I knew I would need to visualize different scenarios for my next race. An ideal visualization would lead me through how to feel in both good and bad race situations.

Midnight Moose 100 Miler - September 2019

I spotted a cute critter on the trail that was the size of a mole and looked like a creature from Pokémon. Oddly enough, the critter didn't run away as I approached. Getting close enough for a good look, I was alarmed when I realized that my critter was nothing more than a rock. Fortunately, I knew what was going on. I had read about runners hallucinating during ultramarathons due to lack of sleep and overexertion. Running for my second full night on the trails, I still had a few hours left before sunrise. It was going to be an interesting night.

***

With five qualifying points under my belt from the QMT, I found another Canadian qualifying race for the UTMB. The Midnight Moose 100 Miler would take place in September in Gatineau Park, just outside of Ottawa, Ontario. If I completed the Midnight Moose I would only need another five points to qualify for UTMB. Midnight Moose was two and a half months away and I had some serious training to do. I wasn't concerned about training volume since I knew that I could put in the work. What concerned me was a demon that I had to confront. After reviewing some of the photos from the QMT, I couldn't ignore that I was overweight.

Dealing with my weight came with a lot of baggage due to my previous struggles. The fact that my weight was holding me back in ultrarunning had been present in the back of my mind for the last two years. I preferred to ignore that fact, though, because weight problems were supposed to be a thing of the past for me. I was ashamed that I needed to lose weight again, but my experience at QMT helped me break through my denial. Although I hadn't prepared properly for the technical terrain at QMT, it was clear that my weight had been the bigger problem. Looking at race photos, I could see that I was carrying excess body fat. Lugging around 220 pounds through the mountains for 110 kilometres was no small feat. Convinced that I didn't want to repeat my difficulties at QMT, I took stock of my current eating patterns.

On most days, I ate three decent-sized meals with a large amount of vegetables. Examining these meals, I didn't see much room for improvement. Portion sizes were reasonable and I was getting a lot of nutrition. The "aha" moment came when I considered my snacks. As funny as it sounds, I was eating a bowl of peanut butter and jam first thing in the morning and again before bed. With three tablespoons of peanut butter and two teaspoons of jam, each snack was 330 calories, for a whopping daily total of 660 calories. What's more, I wasn't even hungry most of the time that I ate the snacks. I vowed to break my snacking habit and stick to eating only three meals per day.

To my delight, I had immediate results and I lost two pounds during the first week that I cut my peanut butter and jam bowls. The pounds continued to melt away as I got closer to race day. Almost three months after QMT, I stepped on the scale and was thrilled to see I had lost 20 pounds. It seemed silly that I had put off dealing with my weight for so long, since I only had to make a small change to my diet. I suspected that shedding 20 pounds was going to have a significant positive impact on my upcoming race; however, I wanted to keep my hopes grounded. A lot can happen over 100 miles.

The Midnight Moose 100 Miler was to take place on a Friday in September at 10:00 p.m. Most 100 milers start early on Saturday mornings, which makes the Midnight Moose unique. Located in Gatineau Park, the start/finish area was at the base of a small ski hill called Camp Fortune. I was excited to explore the area since I had heard great things about the park. Chris had been running there the previous year and had raved about the hilly terrain, rugged trails, and beautiful views.

I was one of the first runners to arrive at Camp Fortune, more than three hours before the 10:00 p.m. start. While walking around the start area, I recognized the race director, Ray Zahab, who was working with his team on some final preparations. Ray is a well-known ultrarunner and adventurer who starred in the 2007 movie, *Running the Sahara*, which was narrated by Matt Damon. He and two friends ran an average of 70 kilometres per day for 111 days to cross the Sahara Desert on foot. Since the movie, Ray has completed several extremely challenging expeditions, including crossing Baffin Island in the Canadian Arctic by himself in January 2020. I took the opportunity to introduce myself to Ray since I knew that he would be very busy getting things ready for the race later. Ray was approachable and took five minutes to chat with me, wanting to know about my running and my background. I was very grateful for my time with Ray and I've become an even bigger fan since meeting him.

After chatting with Ray, the race staff directed me to a camping area near the start line. I set up my tent, assembled all my racing gear, and then tried to get some sleep while more runners arrived. A dull roar had built outside my tent, though, with excited runners talking about the race. Unable to sleep with all the excitement, I emerged from my tent to take in the festive scene. Rows of coloured candles were lit near the start line and several racers wore glow bands.

Before long, it was time to line up for the start of the race and I assembled at the start line with a large group of runners. The 100-mile runners were to start along with runners of the 25-kilometre, 50-kilometre, and 100-kilometre distances. I fell into place mid-pack and lined up beside another 100-mile racer who I recognized as Jeff, a runner who reviews ultramarathons on YouTube. I told Jeff that I recognized him and that I liked his videos. Jeff shrugged off my compliment and I couldn't help feeling snubbed. I didn't have time to dwell on it, though, since we were only a few minutes away from starting.

We surged forward as a group, and racers started their watches. I hadn't heard a countdown but it was clear that the race had started. I began climbing the Camp Fortune ski hill, which is around 150 metres in elevation. Reaching the top of the mountain, we turned downhill, into the woods, and onto some mountain bike single track. Covering around 10 kilometres, I came out of the woods and followed the course onto the road. I ran on a mix of road and relatively flat gravel trails for another 10 kilometres and then got back on the mountain. Climbing a large set of stairs, I reached the top of King Mountain and got a beautiful view of the surrounding area. A vista of twinkling lights greeted me as I gazed out over Ottawa in the distance.

Guided by my headlamp, I ran along the top of the mountain and eventually descended back on a mix of road and gravel trail. Having covered a manageable 18 kilometres, I climbed back into the mountains for the final 32 kilometres of the 50-kilometre loop. I stumbled my way through those technical trails, catching my toe on a rock every few kilometres since it was difficult to see with the light of my headlamp.

The sun had started to peak above the horizon when I ran into the start/finish area for the first time. I finished my first 50-kilometre loop a little after 6:00 a.m. with a time of 8 hours, 4 minutes. During my preparation for the race, I had made two sets of time goals: an aspirational goal and a realistic goal. I beat my realistic goal of 8.5 hours for my first loop and came short of my aspirational goal of 7 hours. Feeling good about my pace, I got a cup of hot coffee from the aid station located near the start line. Loving every sip of coffee, I walked over to my car, changed into dry clothes, and ate two chocolate chip cookies and a peanut butter and jam tortilla for breakfast.

I got back on the trails for my second loop with renewed energy. In fresh running clothes and with a full stomach, I could have been at home going out for my early morning run. As I climbed the Camp Fortune ski hill, I met a racer named Mike who was also in good spirits. With a slim build and short dark hair, Mike had a French Canadian accent and was a few years older than me. We started chatting and decided to pace together without actually discussing it. Mike explained that this was his first ultramarathon and that he was a road marathon runner. I was glad for the company after running alone for most of the night; however, I had been looking forward to listening to music. Wanting to stay focused on the technical trails, I decided to hold off on listening to music until sunrise.

I finally got to put my earbuds in after running with Mike for an hour. Being a marathon runner, Mike couldn't keep up on the more technical section of trail. We decided that I would run ahead and that we would most likely see each other at the next aid station.

After running for over an hour in the woods, I came to the familiar stretch of road that I recognized from the previous loop. I saw a sign at the side of the road indicating that a cross-country ski race was in session. Confused because it was only September, I wondered how someone could ski in these conditions. After running along the side of the road for a few minutes, I was passed by one of the curious cross-country skiers. Like traditional cross-country racers, these athletes used ski poles but they wore long in-line skates in place of skis. The skiers grimaced as they sprinted up hills and tucked low going downhill. At one point, I saw a team of racers in a human train, a group of six skiers made a single-file line and all grasped each other's poles as they zoomed down the hill. Watching the cross-country race was a great distraction from the strain of running and the time flew by on that road section.

True to form, Mike caught up to me, showing his speed on the road. We resumed pacing together, eventually climbing back up King Mountain and getting another great view. The sun glimmered off the Ottawa River in the distance and we could see the Parliament Buildings.

The trails became more technical, with bigger climbs, as we approached the last 20 kilometres of our loop. I pushed the pace since I was eager to see my family who were waiting for me at the start/finish area. Mike explained that he wasn't feeling great and encouraged me to go ahead without him since he wanted to conserve energy. I reluctantly left Mike, although I expected we would meet again at the next aid station.

Feeling good, I covered the last 20 kilometres of the loop in decent time. I came through the finish line at around 3:30 p.m. to the applause from the small group of aid-station volunteers. Once again, my time of 9 hours, 24 minutes fell between my realistic time goal of 10 hours and aspirational goal of 8.5 hours. Although I was short of my aspirational goal, I was happy with my pace. I was on track to finish well before the race's 36-hour cut-off time.

Norah came running from the nearby forest as I walked to the aid station. She was followed by James, David, and my three nephews who are close in age to my kids. Feeling emotional from being on the trails for over 17 hours, I hugged each of the kids as they reached me. Lindsay, and my sister Jacquie, holding my baby niece, also got sweaty hugs when they made their way over to see me. Conveniently, Jacquie and her family only lived a half hour away from Gatineau Park in a suburb of Ottawa.

The children provided some much-needed comic relief. Feeling like we were at a party, the kids helped themselves to the potato chips at the aid-station table. I told the kids that the food was only for racers but the volunteers said that it was okay. I had just finished refilling my water bottle when David took the bottle from my hand and drank almost half of it. David informed me that he was really thirsty from eating the salty chips. After some more laughs, I decided it was time to get back on the course. I felt extremely grateful for my family as I waved goodbye. I was also glad that I got to see my nephew Aidan. Sadly, Aidan had been diagnosed with leukemia in March 2018. I had pledged to complete the Midnight Moose for Aidan and had raised money for the Leukemia & Lymphoma Society of Canada in the weeks prior to the race. I got a little teary as I made my way up the mountain. The raw emotions involved in ultrarunning tend to draw my thoughts to my family and I think about them often while I'm racing.

Adding to my stirring emotions were worries about my second sleepless night on the trails. I had never been up for two nights in a row and I didn't know how my body would react. I calmed my worries by thinking about how Navy SEALs can go a full week without sleep. SEALs are kept awake for most of the night during hell week, the grueling first week of a 24-week training course. If SEALs can go a full week without sleep, I could certainly do two days.

I ran through a low point for around three hours after leaving my family and I struggled to keep pace. I felt like my body was preparing for a much-needed sleep, reacting to the setting of the sun. In addition to feeling low, I hadn't seen anyone on the trail for a long time since the last two aid stations I had passed were unmanned. With only 16 runners in the 100-mile race, the race directors figured that we would be okay with fewer volunteers. Luckily, I passed two attractive ladies who were out hiking with headlamps. They saw my race bib and asked about my run. It was around 7:30 p.m. and I told them that I had been on the trails since 10:00 p.m. the previous night. They told me how impressed they were and encouraged me to keep going. With my mood lifted, I plodded on.

By the time I reached a manned aid station it was pitch dark and I was 20 kilometres into the last loop. The nice lady running the aid station casually mentioned that I was in fourth place. I wasn't sure I had heard her correctly and asked if she could repeat herself. Once again, she said that I was in fourth place. I knew I was near the front of the pack but I didn't realize that I was so close. Although I was tired and sore, I left the aid station feeling great and set a strong pace.

After running for about 10 kilometres, my progress halted when I spotted a curious small animal on the trail. I had come within a few metres of the critter and kept expecting it to scurry off. Finally, walking right up to the animal, I realized that it was not a critter at all. I was staring at a rock. I suspected that I might start hallucinating, since it was my second night in a row without sleep. Making a mental note to be mindful of these visions, I got back on my way. I knew that I needed to be careful so I didn't hurt myself, but I didn't have time to dwell on it. I was in fourth place. I had also read about other ultrarunners hallucinating and knew it was fairly common during longer races. In fact, hallucinations are considered a rite of passage for trail runners. Courtney Dauwalter, one of the world's top ultrarunners, thought she saw a friendly leopard lounging in a hammock during the second night of the 2017 Moab 240 Endurance Run (Trail Runner 2017).

Fortunately, the hallucinations subsided during the short distance to the next aid station and I was glad for another chat with a volunteer. After some small talk, the volunteer shared in a hushed tone that the third-place runner had left the aid station only 10 minutes earlier. On top of that, the volunteer shared that the third-place runner could no longer run and was hiking the rest of the course.

Having never finished an ultramarathon in the top 10, the thought of finishing in third place energized me and I set off on the trails, moving fast. Testing how fast I could run, I managed to hit the same pace that I held for my training runs. Amazed that I could do it, I ran fast and free for the next half hour. I thought about a story that Chris had shared about one of his 100-mile races. He had told me about how great it felt to run fast when you are far into an ultra; it makes you feel invincible. I was experiencing that for the first time and it did feel like nothing could break me.

I finally encountered third place, about an hour after leaving the aid station. I was running fast on a small downhill when I saw third place sitting on a bench off the side of the trail.

"Whoa, you're flying!" he said when he saw me.

"Thanks, I feel good." I said, as I continued running fast.

I realized that third place was Jeff, the same runner who snubbed me at the beginning of the race. I felt a great amount of satisfaction as I passed Jeff, but I couldn't help feeling sorry for him as well. There's a strong sense of camaraderie among ultrarunners and I respected Jeff's efforts. He had been on the trails for over 24 hours, just like I had. We continued chatting as I went by and I made sure that Jeff was okay before I left.

I continued moving fast for another half hour so that Jeff wouldn't catch me. Looking behind me every five minutes or so, I kept thinking that I would see Jeff's headlamp at any moment. I slowed down to a more comfortable pace after another 15 minutes, thinking that I had built a decent buffer on Jeff. Feeling like I was running on autopilot, I did my best to tune out the general pain in my body. My back ached, my thighs were beyond sore, and my feet throbbed. Twenty-six hours of straight running had taken its toll on me.

I was running a particularly dark and technical section when I thought I heard a voice. Stopping for a few seconds and looking into the darkness, I heard the voice again.

"Hello," the voice said.

I thought I might be hallucinating again since I couldn't see anything, but I had never heard about runners hearing things during long races. I said hello back to the voice and it took about 30 seconds before I saw a headlamp come on. Susan, who I had met at the start of the race, materialized about 10 metres off the trail. She was sitting on a stone ledge with her emergency blanket wrapped around her body. Susan was in her early forties and had kept at the head of the pack for most of the race. She explained that her ankle had locked from a bad sprain and that she was calling the emergency numbers without getting anyone. I offered to walk her down the mountain and to give her my emergency blanket and coat but she refused. I was concerned about Susan; however, I was also burning a lot of time. I could picture Jeff coming around the corner at any moment. After offering to assist Susan for a good five minutes, I realized that she might not actually want my help. If that was the case, I could certainly understand how Susan might have been feeling. It was midnight and we still had at least another four hours of running in the dark ahead of us; someone coming to pick me up would have been a great relief.

Susan and I decided that I would keep going to the next aid station and I would send help for her. I wasn't sure if the next aid station was manned, though, and I let Susan know as much. Making it to the aid station 30 minutes later, I was relieved to see two volunteers. I approached the aid station and was greeted by light cheers and then some surprised questions.

"I don't know you. Who are you?" the volunteer said.

"I'm Jordan," I said.

"Where's Jeff?" the volunteer said.

I explained that I had passed Jeff a little while back and then explained about Susan. The volunteer turned out to be Jeff's wife and she was obviously concerned about him. To her relief, Jeff ran into the aid station only a few minutes after I arrived. I was shocked. I had moved into second place when I passed Susan and I didn't want to give that up. I conferred for a few minutes with Jeff and the volunteers to ensure that Susan was going to get help. Assured that first-aid staff was on their way, I filled up my water bottles and prepared to leave. I had a brief conversation with Jeff as I left.

"You had legs of fire out there," said Jeff.

"Thanks, I was feeling good."

"I was not feeling good, but I've started running again since you passed me."

"Glad to hear it," I said.

Getting back on the trail, I was very anxious that Jeff was going to catch me. Jeff didn't seem like he was in much of a hurry, though, and was sitting down at the aid station when I left. Once again, I glanced over my shoulder for the next hour, looking for his headlamp. Jeff never materialized, though, and I relaxed a little as I got closer to the finish line. To light applause, I finished 150 kilometres of running at around 2:30 a.m. The volunteers directed me back on the course for my final 10 kilometres. Running another 10 kilometres seemed like a monumental task, especially since I was so close to my tent and the prospect of lying down for a sleep. To make matters worse, I needed to climb the Camp Fortune ski hill again.

I somehow mustered the willpower to fight the allure of the finish area and I got back on the course. I wasn't going to drop out of the race after running 150 kilometres. Besides, what could go wrong during a 10-kilometre run?

As I climbed, I took special note of the Camp Fortune ski chalet that was located around 25 metres away from the start/finish area. A large banquet-hall-style building, the chalet was brightly lit and I could see a good-sized gathering of men, women, and children in white clothes. Standing outside the chalet, a group of five men formed a circle, all grasping a white sheet. The men threw the sheet into the air and then brought it back down, looking like they were playing a game. I reasoned that it must be a wedding reception that had gone late. I got to the top of the hill and followed the course markers, which sent me back onto the mountain bike single track. Continuing to follow the markers, I arrived at an unfamiliar ski lift at the base of the hill. Slightly panicked, I realized that I had gone off course. Pacing back and forth for a few minutes, I decided to run on the main road back towards the ski chalet, thinking that I must have made a wrong turn in that area.

With panic motivating me, I once again summoned the speed that I had tapped into earlier, running at the same pace as my regular training runs. After running on road for 15 minutes, I arrived at the driveway to the ski chalet and headed toward the wedding guests who were still celebrating outside. As I got closer to the wedding guests, I came to a shocking realization. The partygoers were not people at all—they were long, beige reeds waving in the wind. I looked over to the group of men I had seen earlier and registered that I was simply looking at a piece of machinery covered with a white tarp. Laughing and shaking my head, I continued past the empty ski chalet searching for the course. Although I was concerned about my visions, I knew that I would finish the race within the hour.

I ran past the ski chalet and felt a great sense of relief when I found the trail markers. Backtracking, I located the section where I had made the wrong turn. With my state of mind, I wasn't completely sure that I had run the complete 10-kilometre route. Nevertheless, I ran on since I was concerned that Jeff would overtake me if I spent any more time backtracking.

With mixed emotions, I ran through the finish line of the Midnight Moose at 4:07 a.m. I still wasn't sure if I had run the complete 10-kilometre route; however, I decided that I was going to enjoy the finish anyhow. I finished in 30 hours, 7 minutes, which was good for second place. This was the first time I had ever broken the top 10 in an ultramarathon and it felt amazing. I had a nice chat with the handful of volunteers at the finish line and I could tell they were impressed with my performance. I was used to finishing mid-pack and I relished the looks of admiration on the faces of the volunteers.

I felt like I needed to be upfront about my detour to the race staff and I explained the route that I had taken to complete my 10 kilometres. I half expected to be disqualified; however, the two volunteers smiled and assured me that my route was okay. With great joy, I accepted my shiny belt buckle and then headed over to my tent for some much-needed sleep. As I walked away, a volunteer asked me if I was going to change out of my race gear before I slept. I assured them that I was, when in reality I was planning on collapsing in my tent the moment I unzipped the door. Taking the volunteer's advice, I painstakingly changed into dry clothes and then got into my sleeping bag. I felt like I was staying at the Ritz-Carlton and sleeping in a feather bed. In an instant, I fell into a deep sleep.

I woke up around three hours later and I hadn't moved an inch while I slept. Although my entire body was very sore, I felt refreshed from the short sleep. I hobbled over to the nearby finish area in search of coffee. As I got closer, I noticed my friend Mike sitting in a camping chair near the aid station. I greeted Mike with a big smile but I got a blank look in return. Mike explained that he still had the final 10 kilometres to go but he would not be completing it. I tried to convince Mike otherwise; however, he explained in no uncertain terms that he was dropping out of the race. It was clear that Mike had battled some tremendous low points on his last 50-kilometre loop. Although I was disappointed for Mike, I could sympathize with him. Two sleepless nights in a row and 150 kilometres of running is an extreme amount of stress, especially for Mike's first 100 miler.

Leaving Mike, I was delighted to find fresh coffee. I chatted with volunteers as I filled up my cup. Much to my surprise, I learned that Jeff had dropped out of the race after I left him at the aid station. I thanked the volunteers again, said goodbye, and then returned to my tent and got packed. As I was about to leave, I was surprised to see Susan walking around without any assistance. She had set up her tent in the same area and was preparing to leave. I expected that she would have been in worse shape given that she was med-evaced from the course in the middle of the night. Nevertheless, I was glad that Susan was okay and I said goodbye to her as I walked towards the parking lot.

Feeling exhausted and accomplished, I left the race site and drove to meet my family who were staying at a nearby hotel. I felt like I had solved a great puzzle with this performance. Racing at a lighter weight had allowed me to finally break the top 10 in an ultramarathon. It seemed like such a simple solution to a difficult problem. I imagine that there are simple solutions like this to most of life's challenges. I was excited about my new racing potential and looked forward to the next opportunity to challenge myself with an ultramarathon.

I also felt great about raising money for charity. In the end, I received charitable donations of $2,600 for the Leukemia & Lymphoma Society of

Canada. Tying the Midnight Moose to a charitable cause helped me see my adventure through to the end. Many of my close friends and family had sponsored me and I didn't want to let them down. I also owed it to my nephew Aidan to finish the race. My suffering during the weekend was only a small amount relative to the pain that Aidan had endured during his years of chemotherapy.

About to arrive at the hotel, I reflected on my prospects for running UTMB in 2021. I now had 10 ITRA points and had all of 2020 to earn the additional five points needed to qualify for UTMB. Time was on my side. What could possibly go wrong?

Ultraliving Lessons

Never Give Up

As I'm writing, over a year has passed since I ran Midnight Moose and I'm still surprised that I finished in second place. I've reflected on what made that possible and I haven't come up with anything extraordinary. It wasn't a low-carb diet, fancy running gear, or a training program. In the end, my ability to persevere made the difference.

I didn't move incredibly fast during the race but I never ceased moving. Simply sticking with my pace helped me move up the rankings. I didn't eat one particular type of food but I never stopped eating. Continuing to eat, even when my stomach ached, helped me maintain my energy throughout the race. I finished in second place because I never gave up. Hour after hour, for 30 hours, I continued to hang on.

Preparation is Everything

"Preparation is everything" is a main lesson from *An Astronaut's Guide to Life on Earth*, a book written by Canadian astronaut Chris Hadfield. Hailing from Milton, Ontario, a 20-minute drive from my home, Hadfield is the famous guitar-playing astronaut. He gained international notoriety in 2015 by singing and playing David Bowie's "Space Oddity" on a broadcast from the International Space Station.

Hadfield writes about the power of preparing for likely scenarios during space missions and in life. He goes on to explain that he lives his life preparing for difficult situations that might never happen. It's not time wasted as there is an incredible amount of confidence that comes with thinking through and preparing for likely scenarios.

Taking my preparation for Midnight Moose seriously, I spent a lot of time researching the course. I was determined to avoid the error I had made for QMT—I hadn't done enough research for QMT and as a result had been surprised by the technical course.

Spending hours on Google Maps, I inched my way along the Midnight Moose course, taking notes as I went. After my review of the route, I made a plan of attack, including which sections I would run fast and which sections I would take my time on. The week before the race, I spent 10 minutes reviewing my notes every day and committing them to memory.

I also ran a rocky and technical section of the Bruce Trail for my training runs twice per week for the month before the race. I felt very comfortable on the technical sections of Midnight Moose because of this training.

I spent more time preparing for Midnight Moose than I had for any other race. I recognized there were some variables that were out of my control; however, I chose to focus on what I could control. After my second place finish, I didn't have a shred of regret for all of the time I had invested in my preparation.

FKT

Chris went flying out of the woods, running strong on the snowy course. Was that really him? I hadn't seen Chris for over two hours since his legs cramped and he had let me run ahead. We had run most of the six-hour Fat Ass Trail Run in Batawa together. A challenging course, the Fat Ass Trail Run took place around a small ski hill just outside of wintry Belleville, Ontario. Now at the end of the race, I walked along while Chris caught up and we ran through the finish line together. We shared a third-place finish, with a distance of 52.5 kilometres in 5 hours, 52 minutes.

Finishing side by side with Chris put special emphasis on how far I had come with my running since meeting him five years earlier. Chris has always been a mentor for me and I have learned so much from him over the years. To this day I continue to learn from Chris; however, now it is on the level of peer rather than coach. He's been instrumental in getting me to the point where I can confidently give other ultrarunners advice on training and completing races. I'm very grateful to now call Chris my training partner and I know that we have many running adventures in our future.

The Fat Ass Trail Run took place in November 2019 and, at that point, I'd had two months to recover since the Midnight Moose 100 Miler. I had exciting plans to achieve my goal of running the UTMB in 2021, the year of my 40th birthday. Prior to Midnight Moose, UTMB had changed its entry qualifications and I spent hours figuring out the complex new set of regulations. In the end, I determined that I could gain entry into the 2021 race if I completed one of UTMB's new races in an exotic location, like China, Oman, Argentina, or Spain, in 2020. The UTMB organization granted guaranteed entry to the UTMB in Chamonix for runners who completed a 100-mile race in these new locations. Runners still needed 15 ITRA points; however, the lottery could be bypassed, which was very good news. According to the UTMB website, there were 26,000 applications for the 2019 UTMB and only 2,300 runners were selected to participate.

After much deliberation, Lindsay and I planned a trip to Val d'Aran in Spain so that I could run the new UTMB race there in July 2020. We had been saving travel points with our credit cards and figured out a fairly economical way for our whole family to travel to Spain. Lindsay and I were thrilled that I had a clear path to UTMB in Chamonix for 2021 and that we were organizing a great family trip.

I maintained my regular running after the Fat Ass race and planned to start my UTMB Val d'Aran training plan in March. Since I was on a roll with racing, having finished second and third in the last two races that I entered, I decided to sign up for another ultramarathon in January. The Stride Inside Indoor Track Race would take place in nearby Guelph, Ontario on a 215-metre track. I contacted Chris and Matt about the race and we all signed up to run in circles for six hours.

Putting in a great effort, I finished 294 laps in six hours for a total of 65 kilometres. Gathered with the other racers at the finish line, I was so proud to have my name called as the third-place overall finisher. Chris had a strong showing, with 269 laps for ninth place overall, and Matt completed over 50 kilometres.

Feeling confident, I was expecting the best as I continued my regular training throughout the rest of January. If I was careful and maintained my momentum, I was on track to have a great experience at UTMB Val d'Aran in July.

Everyone is very familiar with what happened as we moved into the spring of 2020. With global cases of coronavirus skyrocketing in March, I feared that my family and I would have to cancel our trip to Spain in July. As expected, UTMB Val d'Aran was eventually cancelled in May 2020 because of

COVID-19. I was saddened by this announcement, though a cancelled race was nothing compared to some of the hardships that people were facing due to the pandemic. Although I was very disappointed, I realized that I was simply postponing my plans to run UTMB and I could still have great ultrarunning experiences close to home.

Still wanting to train for a big running project, I thought about potential fastest known time routes that I could run. As discussed in the opening chapter, fastest known times are a subset of ultrarunning where runners attempt to break speed records on well-known footpaths. The website Fastestknowntime.com is at the heart of the FKT movement. Founded in 2008 by Peter Bakwin, Fastestknowntime.com is the official depository for all speed records. To view a web page of a route on Fastestknowntime.com is to get a history of the record holders over the years. The 3,523-kilometre Appalachian Trail, a premier route located on the east coast of the United States, has 15 speed records displayed on its page. Records include well-known ultrarunners Scott Jurek, who set the supported FKT in 2015 with 46 days, 8 hours, and Karl Meltzer, who subsequently broke Jurek's record in 2016 with a time of 45 days, 22 hours. The current supported record has held since 2018 and was set by Karel Sabbe, a Belgian dentist, with a time of 41 days, 7 hours.

In addition to keeping records, Fastestknowntime.com clearly defines the guidelines for FKTs. The three main types of FKTs are: supported, self-supported, and unsupported. In a supported FKT an athlete can have unlimited help from a crew along his way. Scott Jurek's wife, Jenny Jurek, was the main support for Scott during his 2015 record-setting run. Jenny followed Scott in a large camping van and assisted with all his needs, including food, water, and clothing.

In a self-supported FKT, the athlete arranges all the support by themselves. An athlete can't pre-arrange to have someone come meet them on the trail to bring supplies; however, an athlete might cache supplies on the route, buy supplies from stores, and sleep in hotels, as long as the resources that the athlete uses are readily available for all other athletes.

In an unsupported FKT, an athlete carries all the food and supplies that they need with them the whole time. They can get water from rivers, lakes, and streams but not from stores.

While brainstorming on FKT projects, an attempt of the Bruce Trail speed record kept coming to the top of my list. I remembered learning about a local runner's FKT of the Bruce Trail a few years earlier. Chris introduced me to ultrarunner Adam Burnett in 2018 at the Sulphur Springs 100 Miler. Chris had been friends with Adam for a few years and he told me about Adam's running accomplishments. Adam had completed some of the world's toughest ultramarathons, including Badwater 135 and the Leadville Trail 100 Run. Adam's biggest running accomplishment was setting the FKT on the 890-kilometre Bruce Trail in September 2017. Covering around 90 kilometres per day, Adam completed the rugged Bruce Trail in 9 days, 21 hours.

I'm very fortunate to have Canada's longest footpath, the Bruce Trail, in running distance from my house. I can leave my front door for my morning run and arrive on the Bruce Trail in 15 minutes. The Bruce Trail follows the Niagara Escarpment, the famous rock formation that Niagara Falls flows over. The rugged terrain of the escarpment is both beautiful and punishing. Technical trails with rocks, mud, and rolling hills can take their toll on a runner's knees and ankles and slow progress.

As described earlier in the book, the Bruce Trail starts at the southern tip of eastern Ontario in the Niagara region and runs north all the way to Tobermory, Ontario. The footpath gets its name from the Bruce Peninsula, the land mass that separates Lake Huron from Georgian Bay. I have a special connection with the Bruce Peninsula since I would drive the length of it with my family every summer while I was growing up. Heading to our cottage on Manitoulin Island, my family and I would ride the Chi-Cheemaun, a 111-meter-long passenger and vehicle ferry, from Tobermory to the island at least two times during the summer. Arriving in Tobermory at the northern tip of the peninsula meant the end of a five-hour car ride and a visit to the ice cream shop. Riding the Chi-Cheemaun was always an adventure as a kid. I marveled at how the bow of the ship opened and allowed cars to drive on board. To this day, the Chi-Cheemaun reminds me of a giant whale that swallows cars whole. I'm sure that my familiarity with the Bruce Peninsula and my fond feelings for Tobermory were among the reasons that I kept thinking about a Bruce Trail FKT.

My thoughts eventually led to solid plans, and in the spring of 2020 I put pen to paper and made arrangements for my bid at the Bruce Trail speed record. True, this was a monumental challenge; however, I believed that I might pull it off with some hard work. I made tentative plans to attempt the supported speed record at the end of August and bought a complete set of digital maps to plan my 890-kilometre route. I made a spreadsheet with the likely distances that I could cover each day and wrote out an aggressive training plan.

A few weeks into my training, I developed a nagging pain in both knees that scared me, since I had run for so many years without knee pain. I considered training through the knee pain like I had with other strains in the past. Most of my running injuries up to that point had gone away over time with some extra stretching and icing.

A fateful phone conversation with Adam Burnett helped steer my course of action. Chris had mentioned my FKT plans to Adam and Adam had graciously agreed to speak with me. I asked Adam about his daily mileage on the Bruce, the toughest parts of the trail, and how he'd trained for his speed record. Our conversation eventually led to why Adam wasn't running anymore. He shared that he was hampered by rainy days early in the FKT attempt, which gave him blisters. The blisters changed his running gait, which eventually led to a knee injury that he suffered midway through the FKT. Adam slogged on, despite the injury, and showed amazing grit by finishing the footpath with a heavily bandaged knee. On September 11, 2017, Adam reached the southern terminus of the Bruce Trail and set a new speed record of 9 days, 21 hours, successfully lowering the previous mark by over 13 hours. Completing this amazing task took its toll on Adam, though, as he would need surgery on his injured knee shortly after the FKT. Consequently, Adam hasn't run any ultramarathons since 2017. When I divulged my knee problems to Adam, he counselled that the Bruce Trail wasn't going anywhere and that I should consider putting off my attempt until my knees felt better.

To my disappointment, my knee pain stuck with me for the rest of the summer. Heeding Adam's advice, I made the tough decision to postpone my Bruce Trail FKT attempt to the following summer so that I could be safe. I knew that the Bruce Trail was going to put my body to the test and I didn't want to start the trek with a knee injury.

I also learned about ultrarunner and Toronto native John Harrison Pockler that same summer. John had moved to Canada from Germany in 2016 and was working in Toronto as a consultant. He had some impressive running credentials, including a win at the Niagara Ultra 50 km and a fourth place finish at the Canadian Death Race, both races in 2017. John announced his intention to set a supported FKT of the Bruce Trail in August 2020. I was disappointed that I couldn't make my own bid for the speed record, though I was glad to watch and learn from John's experience.

John started his attempt on September 11th and I eagerly followed his progress report posts on social media. He was running an average of 90 kilometres per day in around 16 hours. I met John on the Bruce Trail just outside of Georgetown on day 8 of his attempt. I knew John's rough location since he was sharing live updates of his GPS tracker through his website. After finishing my work day, I showed up unannounced at a trailhead, hoping that I could pace with John. Shortly after I parked my car, John's crew pulled up in two vehicles, a large camper van and a minivan. I knew from John's social media posts that he had full-time support from two people and occasional support from a third person. I had a nice chat with the crew, dropped off some chocolate chip cookies that Norah had made, and then asked if I could run up trail so that I could pace with John. The crew thought John would be okay with a pacer so I ran on the trail for about 10 minutes before meeting John.

John emerged from the trees, moving fast, and wearing a green long-sleeved shirt and black running pants. He was trailed by another local runner who had joined him earlier as a pacer. John took easy strides while quickly planting his hiking poles to continue his strong pace. I stepped off the trail so that both runners could pass. John politely acknowledged me with a smile and agreed that I could pace with him for a while. I was thoroughly impressed at John's pace; he was running 10-minute kilometres and easily navigating the rocky terrain. John was in good spirits considering he was on his eighth day of running for 16 hours straight. We held a conversation and John mentioned that he had not suffered any major injuries while on the Bruce, despite starting the trek with some nagging leg strains. John mentioned, however, that he was in so much pain in the mountainous Collingwood, Ontario section that he thought he could have broken legs. He also mentioned that he thought it would be interesting to make a self-supported attempt of the Bruce Trail, carrying his own gear and food, and sleeping off the trail. I left John and his pacer after running with them for 30 minutes. We had run into two other trail runners who were waiting to pace with John and I wanted these runners to have their own turn.

I drove back home from the trailhead feeling as inspired as ever to run the Bruce Trail. Two days later, John would finish at the southern terminus in Niagara with a total time of 9 days, 17 hours, successfully claiming the FKT for the Bruce Trail and lowering Adam Burnett's record by only 4 hours.

My first-hand encounter with John certainly left an impression on me. I knew that I would need to put in long days on the trail to have a chance at claiming the FKT; however, I didn't realize that I would need to run for 16 hours per day to do it. Through my conversations with John and his crew, I learned that John was getting up at 5:00 a.m., getting on the trail as soon as he could, and then running until 10:00 p.m. Although I thought I could push myself to do that, I knew I would enjoy a more humane FKT attempt. Thinking through my options, I realized that a self-supported FKT attempt would allow me more leeway to enjoy the trail without pushing my body to its max.

At this time, the self-supported Bruce Trail FKT was held by Charlotte Vasarhelyi, who completed a 16-day, 21-hour north to south journey of the Bruce Trail on August 15, 2016. Vasarhelyi is a native of nearby Kitchener, Ontario, who has many impressive running accomplishments. She previously held the outright Bruce Trail FKT for men and women in 2010 with a time of 13 days, 10 hours. In 2018, Vasarhelyi came in fourth place for women at the grueling Moab 240. During her 80 hours and 55 minutes on the trail, Vasarhelyi crossed 240 miles of desert and canyons and two mountain ranges. I haven't found detailed background material on Vasarhelyi's self-supported FKT of the Bruce Trail other than a short write-up with some photos on Facebook. The write-up describes unusually hot weather and the side trips that Vasarhelyi made to find water and food. Unlike most of the Bruce Trail speed records that are set in the early fall, Vasarhelyi completed her Bruce Trail end-to-end wearing a backpack in the heat of early August. I have never met Vasarhelyi, though I noticed we both ran the 6-hour Horror Trail Race in 2018. While it has no bearing on whether or not I can complete a Bruce Trail FKT, I was pleased to see that I beat Vasarhelyi in the race, coming in 11th place to her 16th.

I continued making loose plans for my Bruce Trail FKT attempt as the last few months of 2020 passed. At the end of December, I shared my plans of a self-supported FKT attempt with Ray Zahab during a phone conversation. Ray and I had kept in touch since I ran his race, the Midnight

Moose, in 2019, and we'd been having short phone conversations every few months. I'm very fortunate to have Ray as a resource since he has so much expedition experience. In addition to his famous completion of running the 7,500-kilometre Sahara Desert in 2006, Ray has completed a large number of expeditions in some of the world's harshest environments. In 2009, Ray broke the speed record for an unsupported expedition to the South Pole on foot and on snowshoes. In 2011, Ray became the first person to run the 1,200-kilometre Atacama Desert in Chile. Fast forwarding to January 2020, Ray crossed Baffin Island on foot in five days while dragging all his supplies in a sled. In addition to these impressive feats, I can easily name another dozen remarkable expeditions that Ray has completed.

I could tell that Ray was excited by the idea of my self-supported FKT attempt of the Bruce Trail. Most of Ray's recent expeditions were self-supported or unsupported and he was passionate about this style of trek. As we discussed Charlotte Vasarhelyi's current self-supported speed record of the Bruce Trail, Ray asked me about the unsupported record. I shared that I hadn't been able to find any documentation of an unsupported record.

"That's how you should do it," said Ray.

"Really?" I asked, "Do you think I could do it unsupported?"

Ray absolutely thought I could do it. He said that a big, strong guy like me should be able to carry a pack with all my necessary gear for the length of the trail. I was excited by the idea; however, I explained to Ray that I had never attempted any sort of trek longer than two days and those were races that were fully supported by aid stations. Ray told me not to worry, he would help me with all the gear that I needed and in the planning of my FKT attempt.

With the vote of confidence from Ray, I went about planning for an unsupported Bruce Trail FKT attempt. I determined to make my attempt in the first two weeks of September when the weather was cooler. In addition to developing and following a solid training plan, I would need to buy all the gear necessary for this ambitious project. As the months went by, I gathered my gear under Ray's guidance and bought an ultra-light tent, sleeping bag, sleeping mat, and backpack. I was amazed that this gear, which would be my home on the trail, only weighed a total of 7.4 pounds.

As a dry run for my FKT attempt, I planned a full weekend trek on the Bruce Trail in early July 2021. I resolved to carry all my gear on a 130-kilometre out-and-back hike from Georgetown to just outside of Orangeville, a small city that is a 40-minute drive north of Georgetown.

The months went by and my training and preparation continued, until the time arrived for my hiking adventure trial run. After leaving my car at the trailhead, I set out from Limehouse Conservation Area at 3:00 a.m. in the complete darkness on a Saturday in early July. I was carrying around 30 pounds in my backpack, which included four litres of water, food, camping gear, and even a 500 millilitre soft flask of red wine. I couldn't run with such a heavy pack so I kept to a fast hike and covered ground quickly. Although the hiking was slower than my usual running pace, I still covered around 75 kilometres in roughly 16 hours. I was very happy to arrive at the Starbucks in a small town called Mono Mills at 7:30 p.m., 30 minutes before closing time. Stopping at Starbucks was a key part of my plan, since I needed to refill my water for making dinner that night and for the next day's hike back home. After refilling my water bottles in the washroom and buying a grande, coffee-free Frappuccino, which is basically a milkshake, I got back on the trail and found a nice campsite. I set up camp, made dinner, drank my soft flask of wine, and with a full stomach and a tired body, I fell asleep to the sound of coyotes howling in the distance.

I got up the next morning at 5:00 a.m. and proceeded to break camp and make breakfast. I ate some oatmeal, drank a coffee, and then set out on the trail on a modified route towards home. After hiking 60 kilometres, I reached my final destination, an ice cream shop in Glen Williams, a small town outside of Georgetown. I sat eating a triple-scoop cookies and cream ice cream cone while waiting for Lindsay to come and pick me up. I was pleased when I finally arrived back home after another long day on the trails. My dry-run hike had more than served its purpose, as it gave me a great sense of a reasonable daily kilometre goal and allowed me to test all my gear.

While I had originally hoped to hike the entire length of the Bruce Trail unsupported, this hike gave me a clearer picture of the difficulties I would be facing. I would have to get all my water from rivers and streams, which gave me significant worry. I was confident that my filter bottles would get rid of bacteria and parasites but they would not get rid of pesticides and heavy metals. Although it was difficult to find any data on the quality of the water along the Bruce Trail, I was wary of the water sources since industries and farmland surround large stretches of the Bruce Trail. In addition to the hazards of drinking water, I would need to carry all my food with me from day 1. From the amount of food that I consumed over the weekend, I knew I would need around two pounds of sustenance each day. I thought it would take me at least 14 days to hike the Bruce Trail, which meant I would need to carry 28 pounds of food in addition to water and all my gear. I also preferred having the option to buy food, water, and supplies from stores along the trail in case I needed anything. Given the difficulties I would be facing and the fact that this was my first long hike, I decided to give myself a break and change my attempt to a self-supported FKT.

Having settled on a self-supported FKT attempt, I got busy with preparations, mindful of my impending start date in early September. After in-depth review of my route, I planned to hike roughly 65 kilometres per day, which would allow me to complete the Bruce Trail in 13 days, 12 hours. I had a clear goal, a plan, and some experience on the trail. What I didn't know, however, were the challenges that awaited me on what was certain to be a great adventure.

Ultraliving Lessons

Don't Worry If You're Worried

The Bruce Trail FKT attempt scared me. I was scared that I would get injured and that I wouldn't have the fortitude to put in the 13 full days of running to set an FKT. Although I was scared, I reminded myself that I'd felt like this during previous important moments in my life. When I ran my first 100-mile race in 2018, I was scared that I would get extremely dehydrated like when I ran the Sulphur Springs course. I chose to harness the nervous energy, though, and turn it into action in the form of training and planning. Using my worries as motivation led to the successful completion of my first 100-mile race.

I adopted my mindset about nervous energy from my grandfather John "Jack" Parry, or Pop as our family called him. Among many impressive achievements, Pop was the starting running-back for the Royal Canadian Air Force football team that won the Grey Cup in 1942 and he also represented Canada in track and field at the 1948 Olympics. Pop died of cancer in 1990 when I was nine years old; however, his wisdom has lived on through our family. Growing up, when my sisters and I would share with my mom that we were feeling nervous about an upcoming event, mom would tell us that it's a good thing we were feeling nervous. She would assure us that Pop always said that you needed to worry if you were not feeling nervous. Pop believed that nerves were your body's way of telling you that something important was coming up.

Pop's lesson has held true through my own life experiences and I've found that nerves, if harnessed correctly, can help you train more effectively, run faster, and perform better. Rather than avoiding my feelings of being nervous and scared about my Bruce Trail FKT attempt, I chose to use those feelings as fuel for all the preparations needed for a successful project.

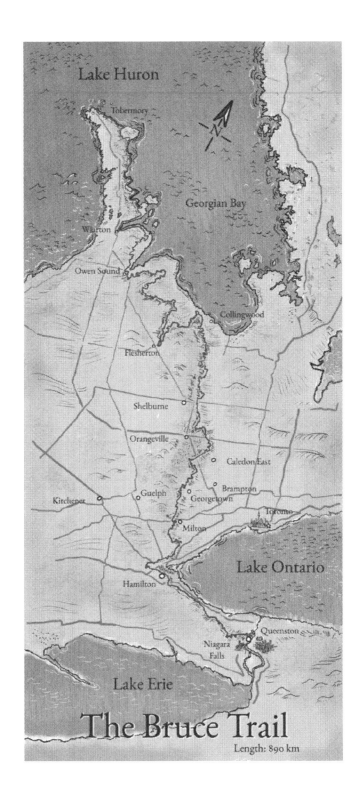

Bruce Trail FKT Attempt (Part 1) – August 2021

I had been sleeping for a few hours when a large crash of thunder woke me with a start. With my thoughts racing, I considered the options that could get me out of my treacherous situation. I could pack up the tent I was currently lying in and brave the thunderstorm that was raging outside, or I could go back to sleep and risk a number of threats. I was camped at the bottom of a ravine on a rock face in the middle of a small river. Surrounded by trees, I held my breath every time I heard a thunder crash, expecting that a large tree limb would fall and obliterate my tent. To make matters worse, rain fell incessantly, causing the river that surrounded my rock face to rise. I had no idea if I was camped in the middle of a river's spillway and I worried that my tent could be washed away by a flood at any minute. This was certainly not how I envisioned the first night of my self-supported Bruce Trail FKT attempt.

***

The day before, I had set off from the southern terminus of the Bruce Trail in Queenston in the early morning. Lindsay and I had stayed over in a hotel room with our kids the previous night, and in the morning everyone piled into the car so they could drop me off at the trailhead near the Canada/US border. With a bittersweet feeling, I said goodbye to my three children while they stayed inside the car. At 5:30 a.m., the kids were barely awake but they did their best to muster smiles for me as I gave each one of them a hug. I proceeded to stand with Lindsay in front of the Bruce Trail's southern terminus cairn for a few minutes, embracing her tightly and telling her how much I was going to miss her. The cairn, at nine feet tall and four feet wide, is an impressive structure, a monument that well-represented what a massive undertaking it is to walk the entire Bruce Trail. As Lindsay and the kids drove away, I got on my way, hiking through the darkness with a strong sense of trepidation and excitement.

Weighing around 40 pounds, my backpack was loaded to its capacity. I carried all my camping gear, three days' worth of food, and four litres of water. Despite this heavy weight on my back, I moved at a good pace and I covered roughly eight kilometres before I felt a big splash of water on my lower back. With alarm, I quickly removed my pack and noticed that the drinking tube had somehow come out of my hydration bladder. I immediately plugged the leak with my finger while I surveyed the damage. My heart sunk when I saw that I had lost two of my four litres of water. Now 7:00 a.m., the temperature was already hot and sticky and I was sweating profusely. From reviewing weather reports before my trip, I knew that it was going to be one of the hottest days of the year. I shrugged off this mishap as bad luck; however, the event was a harbinger of things to come.

Being mindful of my water consumption, I continued plodding along, travelling west towards a town called Thorold. In the mid-morning, I caught up to a couple in their mid-sixties who were donned in hiking gear from head to toe. I had a brief conversation with the couple as I passed, since they had asked me about my backpack and my final destination.

"I'm going to Tobermory," I stated, proudly.

I received admiring smiles in return and some advice on where I could fill up my water bottles over the next 20 kilometres. The man had done most of the talking but the lady piped up as we were about to part ways.

"Do you know how to spot poison ivy?" she asked.

I assured her that I was very familiar with poison ivy and its harmful effects.

"Well, you're standing in it," she said.

Sure enough, I was standing in a small patch of poison ivy. I had stepped off the trail to allow the couple to pass and didn't notice the three-leaved devil plants. Fortunately, my lower legs were completely covered by my calf sleeves and the poison ivy didn't touch my skin. Sheepishly, I thanked the lady for pointing out the poison ivy and made a mental note that I'd need to wipe down my shoes and calf sleeves before bed.

I set off on the trail again after that brief conversation and the temperature rose steadily as the morning progressed to noon. My water supply continued to worry me since I was sweating so much—I had soaked my T-shirt and shorts. I carried water filters with me, but I remained wary of drinking water from natural sources since I was so close to Hamilton, one of Canada's largest industrial cities. I have made a point to eat as much organic food as possible over the last many years and I didn't want to undo all my good work with a litre or two of chemical-infused water.

With a sense of relief, I finally reached my first water drop at the Short Hills Provincial Park. Lindsay and I had stopped there the day before on our way to our hotel and I had hidden a three-litre plastic jug of water in some long grass behind a telephone pole. After a short search, I pulled my water jug from its hiding spot and felt a great sense of relief that it was still there. I filled my empty hydration bladder, double-checking that the drinking tube was secure, and then strapped the empty bottle to my pack so that I could throw the jug in the first garbage that I encountered.

By that time, it was a little after 2:00 p.m. and I had covered 35 kilometres, around five kilometres less than my predetermined pace. I had planned on covering five kilometres per hour but the heat had slowed me down. The temperature had risen past 30°C and the sun was now out in full force. I pushed on towards my next water drop, which was 30 kilometres away, and surmised that if I stayed on my planned pace, I should reach it by around 8:00 p.m.

Despite my best efforts, my progress slowed down significantly due to the technical terrain and heat. Around 6:30 p.m., I realized that I wasn't going to make it to my second water drop as I had only covered another 15 kilometres. At that point, I was walking a long stretch of country road and I noticed a lone figure sitting on a chair outside of a farmhouse. Desperate for water, I walked up the gravel driveway and asked the figure if he had an outdoor hose that I could use to fill up my bottles. When I got close enough to read the man's facial expressions, I realized that he couldn't understand what I was saying. Having grown up in a farming community, I knew that migrant workers from Mexico often work on Ontario farms during the growing season. I tapped in to my limited Spanish vocabulary and asked the man in the chair for "agua." With a head nod, the man disappeared into the house and, after a few minutes, he emerged with another man who carried four small plastic bottles of water. I graciously accepted the water, and with smiles and waves I made my way back onto the country road. I felt that everything was right in the world after being the recipient of this generosity from two men who had travelled to Canada for work.

I made my way back into the forest and hiked until the sun had almost set, around 8:15 p.m. Since it was my first day on the trail, I wanted to have some sunlight for setting up camp. Racing against the sunset, I chose my precarious campsite on the rock face, surrounded by water and at the bottom of a ravine. I was happy to be near a water source, although I would come to regret my decision later that night. I was exhausted from the long day and made the questionable decision to eat a few snacks rather than have a proper dinner.

I was scared for my life when the thunderstorm woke me a few hours later. Sheets of rain fell and the wind shook my tent. I spent a tense hour waiting for the weather to improve but the storm raged on. Unzipping my tent, I emerged and examined the surrounding water with my headlamp. There was no doubt that the water levels were rising and the sound of the current upstream was getting louder. Could I have even chosen a worse campsite? My surroundings looked very much like a spillway and I expected that my tent would be washed away at any second by a rush of water. I considered packing up my tent and hiking through the night, but thoughts of getting hit by a falling tree branch or getting struck by lightning held me back.

Despite my fears, I got back into my tent and lay on my air mattress with eyes open, listening for the oncoming rush of water that would spell my doom. I emerged from my tent after another 30 minutes of intense rain and once again examined water levels. To my relief, the streams that broke around my rock face had not gained any more volume. Thunder and lightning continued to strike but the storm had finally lost some of its intensity. I got back in my tent and despite all the danger I managed to sleep for a few hours before getting up at 4:30 a.m. in dark but clear skies.

I had only hiked 53 kilometres the previous day, which was well short of my 65 kilometre per day goal. Resolved to make up time, I decided against boiling water for the coffee and oatmeal I had brought with me for breakfast.

I had hung my shorts, T-shirt, socks, and underwear from the previous day on tree branches to dry overnight and each piece of clothing was soaked from the rain when I went to retrieve them. I had only brought one T-shirt and one pair of shorts and I shivered as I put them on. My one pair of dry underwear was my saving grace since I had packed two pairs of quick-dry underwear. I tied the wet pair of underwear to my backpack so that it could dry during the day. It was an exercise in humility to display my underwear for everyone to see.

I finished breaking camp and then set off on the trail from just outside of the hilariously named Ball's Falls Conservation Area. I reached my next water drop after an hour of hiking and I made good progress for the next few hours even though the terrain was challenging. After passing the town of Thorold, the trail had long stretches of single track that cut through the middle of the escarpment. I expended a lot of energy hiking the ups and downs of the escarpment, all while watching my footing on the rocky terrain. The escarpment is set back a few kilometres from Lake Ontario and I enjoyed views of the shoreline when I came upon lookouts.

I had drank all my water but I wasn't overly thirsty by the time I reached my next water cache just outside of a town called Beamsville. Although the temperature had risen steadily since the morning, I had kept cool on the shaded trails. My day continued without any mishaps and I hiked through the town of Grimsby in the mid-afternoon. I began to slow down as twilight set in—my calorie deficit had caught up with me and I needed some real food. Determined to have a better night than the previous one, I stopped hiking at around 7:30 p.m. and found a decent campsite. I was happy with my progress for the day, 62 kilometres, and I was looking forward to a hot meal. I had packed a small butane stove and I used it to boil the water that I added to a freeze-dried dinner package of sweet and sour pork with rice. I savoured the hot food and my body instantly reacted to the influx of calories. I went to bed that night feeling much better than the night before.

I was greeted by a pair of shining yellow eyes when I unzipped my tent at 4:30 a.m. the next morning. I couldn't make out the full details of the animal that stood around 20 metres away from me, but I was pretty sure I was looking at a coyote. I was unnerved that the coyote didn't run away when it first saw me, so I yelled, "hey" and, "get out of here." Unaffected by my yelling, the coyote continued to stand its ground but it didn't come any closer. Being mindful of my time, I continued breaking camp and hoped that the coyote would eventually lose interest and leave. The coyote wasn't my only surprise that morning; I also had to deal with the disappearance of the underwear I had tied to my backpack the day before. To my dismay, I couldn't find the undergarment anywhere and figured that it must have fallen off my pack during my travels. After a fruitless search, I begrudgingly accepted that I would have to hike in one pair of underwear for the rest of my trek. Fortunately, I had one additional pair of cotton underwear that I wore only for sleeping.

After eating a hot breakfast and finishing with breaking camp, I scanned the forest with my headlamp and was glad that I didn't see any sign of the coyote. I set off into darkness, singing as I went in an effort to ward off any dangerous animals. Gordon Lightfoot's "The Wreck of the Edmund Fitzgerald" was my song of choice since I easily remembered all the lyrics. I had sung Lightfoot's classic to help put my kids to sleep when they were babies.

I had hiked a few more hours on the tough terrain of the escarpment when I came across Felker's Falls just outside of Hamilton. I was struck by the beauty of the cascading water and spent some time appreciating the view from the trail. At 22 metres in height, Felker's Falls is around half the height of Niagara Falls. Energized by my surroundings, I picked up the pace as I made my way into Hamilton on much easier terrain. With a population of around 537,000 people, Hamilton is the largest city on the Bruce Trail.

The trail turned into a paved walkway and I easily navigated the kilometres through the outskirts of the city. As I walked, I thought about a phone conversation I'd had with Lindsay the previous day. She asked if I could run for a few hours each day to make up time. I told Lindsay that my pack was too heavy and I couldn't do it; however, I felt compelled to test out Lindsay's suggestion while I was on easier terrain. I started with a slow jog and was pleased that I could hold this pace for 15 minutes without much trouble. I decided to push on with my running, backing off if I needed to. I kept up my slow jog as I made my way onto dirt trails through the forested areas of Hamilton. Now mid-morning, I had completely run out of water and was worried about my prospects for the day. As I ran along with my slow shuffle, I was passed by a trail runner who was out for his morning run. I took a long shot and called out to the runner, asking him if he knew where I could fill up my water. To my surprise, he told me that I simply needed to walk about 50 metres to a public fountain on the street. I was skeptical, but I took the runner's advice and was delighted to find the fountain exactly where he said it was located. I filled my flask and then quickly guzzled it, enjoying the cold water. I repeated this process two more times before filling my hydration bladder and making my way back onto the trail. With water sloshing in my stomach, I continued my slow run through Hamilton and felt great about the progress I was making with my new mode of transportation. It had turned into a beautiful day and I enjoyed being among the many people who were hiking the trail. As I came out on the west side of Hamilton, I passed over Highway 403, one of Canada's busiest highways, at around 1:30 p.m. I certainly noticed the curious juxtaposition of the busyness of the highway compared to the calm and serene nature of the trail.

After two more hours of running and hiking, I reached the Dundas Valley Conservation Area, the site of the annual Sulphur Springs trail race. I felt a great sense of nostalgia as I ran through familiar sections of the course, and I conjured the excitement from my first 100-mile race that had taken place there three years earlier. After covering the roughly 10 kilometres of trail through the conservation area, I emerged onto a road as I began my route through the town of Dundas. I took some time to study my electronic Bruce Trail map that I kept on my phone and noticed and that I would be passing only one block north of downtown Dundas. Since it was close to the end of the day, I decided to make the short trip downtown to look for a place to eat dinner. I settled on a restaurant called Café Domestiique, which was situated on a street corner and had a large stretch of windows at the front of the restaurant.

I was reading the menu affixed near the front door when a man knocked on the window and gestured for me to come in. The man introduced himself as Krys and I could tell that he had a warm and jovial personality after only a few minutes of conversation. Krys appeared to be in his late forties and he wore a Dundas Valley T-shirt, which is the section of the trail I had hiked earlier that day. I mentioned to Krys that I didn't have a lot of time so he suggested a pre-prepared chicken dish that was served with some toasted baguette. I told Krys that I would take two of those dinners along with a pint of beer. I drank my beer and ate my meals in the outside courtyard, savouring everything. Eating prepared food and sitting at a table was a real treat after three full days on the trail. As I finished my meal, Krys brought me two large scones and told me they were for tomorrow's breakfast. Although I only stayed for a short time, I was touched by the hospitality I received at Café Domestiique.

As I got back on the trail, I noticed I was feeling more buzzed than usual after drinking only one beer. I didn't mind the feeling, since my buzz had a nice pain-dulling effect on my feet, knees, and back that were sore from the long days on the trail. By the time I got back into a forested area, it was close to sunset and I was once again thinking about where I would camp for the night. I had surveyed my Bruce Trail map while I was eating dinner and found a nice-looking camping area outside of a place called Rock Chapel. Propelled by my beer buzz, I started running again, now towards my camping destination. I found a field of long grass that was perfect for setting up camp, though I was concerned about wood ticks since long grass is one of the preferred habitats for the blood-sucking insects. I started worrying about more than ticks when I saw a recently shed snakeskin right beside the corner of my tent. My mind went to dark places even though I knew there weren't any rattlesnakes on that section of the Bruce Trail.

Doing my best to put my worries aside, I got into my tent and started tending to my sorry-looking feet. I had painful blisters on the sides of my heels and on the balls of my feet, and I took the time to drain each of these blisters. The process took a long time since I needed to clean my feet with baby wipes, wipe each of the blisters with an alcohol swab, and then cut a small hole into each blister with the tiny pair of scissors from my Swiss Army knife. A sewing needle would have been much better for the job of popping blisters, but I had overlooked packing a needle in my last few days of preparation. Being very mindful of potential infection, I sterilized my small pair of scissors by holding the blades over the flame from my lighter for 30 seconds or so each time I used them. I would become very familiar with this foot-care routine over the next few days.

I awoke with a headache and a rumbling stomach the next morning and immediately ran a mental diagnostic on what I had done the day before that could have led to my current condition. It didn't take long for me to realize that my symptoms felt very similar to a hangover and I immediately regretted drinking the pint of beer with last night's dinner. I reasoned that I couldn't handle the extra stress of processing alcohol since my body was already under so much stress from the long days on the trail. Swearing off beer for the rest of my trek, I began my fourth day on the Bruce Trail, travelling east towards

Burlington, the large city located on the northern shore of Lake Ontario, right across from Hamilton. I had covered a respectable 63 kilometres the previous day and planned on travelling another 65 kilometres so I could make it to the city of Milton.

Although I didn't feel great, I was moving well and resumed my slow run like the day before. After a few hours, I came upon Grindstone Creek, a beautiful area near Waterdown, a small town to the northwest of Burlington. While in Grindstone Creek, I ran beside a picturesque and fast-flowing river and took special note of an area beside the river that had more than 40 inukshuks. These human-like stone structures were all shapes and sizes, some a few inches tall whereas others were a few feet tall. I would later learn that locals called this area the inukshuk village.

As morning turned to mid-day, I found myself travelling on a five-kilometre stretch of road that led to the Mount Nemo Conservation Area. I was in the familiar predicament of being out of water and I decided to once again look for a resident who might be able to give me some water. I had almost reached Mount Nemo and was about to give up hope when I saw a lady emerge from her house and get into her car. I walked up her driveway, waved to get her attention, and politely asked if she had an outdoor hose for me to fill up my water. She told me that she would be happy to fill my water but she needed to leave for an appointment and she would ask her husband to help me. The lady's husband introduced himself as Bob and I learned that he was also a runner who had spent a lot of time on his local section of the Bruce Trail. Bob graciously filled my hydration bladder and wished me luck as I continued running down the road.

After a short hike, I arrived at the Mount Nemo Conservation Area, which is on the northern outskirts of Burlington. At 290 metres in elevation, Mount Nemo is challenging to climb, especially in the heat of the day. I took it slow and watched my footing as I navigated the jagged rocks and narrow switchbacks. I was rewarded for my efforts with a terrific view of the Greater Toronto Area once I reached the lookout at the top of the mountain. It was such a clear day that I could even see the CN Tower, in the distance, in downtown Toronto over 60 kilometres away.

I carried on, hiking through Crawford Lake and Rattlesnake Point, two conservation areas that I am familiar with since they are close to my home in Georgetown. I was surprised to meet Jack on the trail in the late afternoon just outside of the Kelso Conservation Area near Milton. Like me, Jack was thru-hiking the Bruce Trail and we had met the day before near Hamilton. Jack certainly got my attention when we met. In his early twenties, Jack wore shoulder-length dreadlocks and a beige bucket hat with a Bruce Trail logo. Jack had greeted me with a smile when we met but I could tell that he had something on his mind. He had only stuck around long enough to explain his thru-hike and then proceeded to leave me in the dust as he set an aggressive pace up the trail. Now meeting a day later, Jack and I greeted each other like old friends and decided that we would share some kilometres on the trail.

I was grateful for Jack's company because I hadn't had any meaningful in-person conversations since I started my trek. I learned more about Jack's backstory. He explained that the hike was his attempt to figure out what to do next in his life since he could no longer play competitive baseball. A former pitcher, Jack had planned on playing minor league baseball before he injured his shoulder. Jack's injury prevented him from carrying a tent and camping gear in a backpack so he slept in his car most nights. Every day, Jack hiked roughly 20 kilometres out and then 20 kilometres back to his car. I was surprised to hear that Jack was hiking the trail this way and suggested that he should hide a bike in the woods at his end point and use the bike to get back to his car every day. Jack told me that he liked my idea, yet I could tell that he was happy with his current methodology. I didn't realize until later that Jack's way of hiking would allow him to complete a yoyo of the Bruce Trail, technically walking the whole 890 kilometres north and then the 890 kilometres south. Yoyos are held in high regard among thru-hikers and I certainly respected what Jack was attempting to do.

As we continued our conversation, I learned that Jack made hip hop music under his artist name of Forest Gumption. As a long time hip hop fan, I was impressed that Jack created his own music and I vowed to download some of his tracks. Our conversation eventually turned to why Jack wasn't feeling very talkative the first time we met and Jack admitted that he had indulged in one too many beers the night before. Jack was mad at himself since he was feeling sluggish, and part of the reason why he was hiking was so that he could improve his health. I could sympathize with Jack. At his age, I had also felt frustrated on several mornings after having too many drinks the night before. Before we knew it, an hour had passed and it was time for Jack to turn back towards his starting point from earlier in the day. We snapped a quick selfie together and exchanged Instagram handles so that we could stay in touch. I was sad to lose a hiking buddy but I was glad to start running again, since I still had a ways to go to reach my final destination for the day.

The sun had almost set when I made it to the top of the escarpment at Kelso, the conservation area just outside of Milton that I often visit with my family. I was tired and famished at that point; however, I still had an hour to hike to reach my water cache. I had driven to Kelso the week before, only a 20-minute drive from my house, to hide four litres of water in the woods.

As I navigated the trails in the pitch dark, only guided by my headlamp, I called Lindsay and complained that I was exhausted. She sympathized with me and encouraged me to keep going. I found it hard to keep up my spirits up once the sun went down. Lindsay and I talked for a good half an hour, and I felt better from the conversation as I emerged from the forest at the base of Kelso's ski hill.

At the exact same moment, I realized that I had to climb straight up the 320 metres of the ski hill to get to my water stash. In my exhaustion, I had forgotten that I needed to emerge from the trail at the top of the mountain to get to my water. Climbing the mountain was the last thing I wanted to do, but I needed my water for cooking so I trudged back to the top of Kelso. I found my water after a short search and brought it with me onto a wooden platform that is used to start downhill ski races in the winter. The wooden structure was rectangular and around 60 feet in diameter. A low wooden fence surrounded the platform, which protected it from the wind. I felt like the platform made a great camping area and I got to work setting up my tent and then boiling water for my supper. I had a spare freeze-dried meal with me from the night I had eaten at Café Domestiique, and I decided that I would eat two meals that night.

After waiting the compulsory eight minutes for my meals to cook, I took the steaming meals into my tent and sat, happily gorging myself on spaghetti and meat sauce and pasta primavera with vegetables. Feeling very satisfied after eating every morsel of food, I started with my routine of foot care so that I could get to bed. The blisters on my heels had drained nicely, but the blisters on the balls of my feet had migrated forward, getting closer to my toes, which made them even more painful. Similar to the night before, I painstakingly drained these blisters after washing my feet and then applied Polysporin with some Band-Aids to allow the blisters to heal overnight. Having finished with my foot care, I gratefully slipped into my sleeping bag and dozed off while pondering what the next few days had in store for me. Although I'd had a few mishaps, my trek was going well and I expected it to continue this way. The Bruce Trail had different plans for me, however, as I would find out over the next few days.

Ultraliving Lessons

Follow Your Dreams

In the weeks prior to my Bruce Trail FKT attempt, I could have postponed my trek due to any number of perceived obstacles: I had a sore foot, I was scared about contracting COVID-19, and I was concerned about being away from my young kids for two weeks. My trepidation built to a crescendo on our drive to the southern terminus in Niagara Falls, the day before I started my trek. Although I was at the height of fear and excitement, I managed to squeeze in a few hours of sleep in our hotel room before waking up at 4:30 a.m. to make my final preparations. Loading my backpack felt surreal while I watched my family sleeping in their beds. Later that morning, I summoned the courage to leave my family and to begin my journey on the Bruce Trail even though I was extremely nervous.

I didn't have all the answers when I set off from the southern terminus in Queenston that morning. I knew it was going to be difficult to find water, I questioned whether I had packed enough food, and I didn't know where I was going to sleep every night. However, I did know that I was following my dreams and I trusted in my ability to make good decisions and to reason my way through difficult challenges. I was also going to need some lucky breaks.

"When you want something, all the universe conspires in helping you achieve it" is one of the main messages from Paulo Coelho's brilliant book *The Alchemist*. Although I would face significant challenges on the trail, I would be helped along on my journey by people and circumstances that I couldn't have planned. I was grateful to have been given water by the nice people that I met on the trail, for the hospitality I was shown by Krys at the Café Domestiique, and for Jack's company. I believe that good things happen when you follow your dreams.

Bruce Trail FKT Attempt (Part 2) - September 2021

The small flame on my camp stove had somehow grown large enough to engulf my entire cooking pot. I smelled the acrid fumes of burning plastic and finally realized that my cooking pot had caught fire; I was burning the plastic container that fit like a sleeve around my cooking pot. I quickly extinguished the stove, slid the burning plastic off my pot, and flung the flaming mess into the grass. Luckily, there weren't any large plastic deposits left on my pot and I could continue boiling water for my breakfast without any fire hazards.

I made coffee and took the time to savour it—my morning cup had become one of my favourite parts of the day. Hot coffee on the trail was a special treat and I always felt energized after my cup of java. I also found the scones that Krys had given me two nights earlier from the Café Domestiique in Dundas. The scones still tasted fresh and were a great change from the oatmeal I had been eating for breakfast every day.

Despite my rocky start with breakfast, I felt refreshed from the night's sleep and excited to start my day. I would be hiking through my home trails near Georgetown and I had an aggressive distance goal for the day. I needed to hike 70 kilometres to get to the Forks of the Credit Inn, where I had rented a room for the night and had a supply box waiting for me. I knew that I had a significant task ahead of me since it had taken me 16 hours the previous day to cover 69 kilometres.

After a thorough clean up, including throwing the melted plastic into a nearby garbage can, I made my way out of Kelso Conservation Area. The trail passed beside a large parking lot and I greeted two workers as they arrived for their early shifts at the conservation area. I was glad for my early start, and also that I didn't meet any of the workers while I was preparing my breakfast.

After an hour's progress, I came across a clearing and enjoyed a beautiful view of the sunrise. A dark orange band stretched across the horizon and I could see the Toronto cityscape in the distance, along with the outline of the mountain at Kelso. I felt giddy as I took in my surroundings. I realized how big of a departure these days were from my normal routine and I felt a deep sense of gratitude for my adventure.

I continued along the trail, leaving the clearing and eventually travelling through an underpass so that I could cross Highway 401, one of North America's most travelled highways. I hiked for another hour before I got onto familiar trails, I was only a 20-minute drive from my home in Georgetown. I made great progress and I enjoyed the feeling of being close to home, although the proximity made me miss my family. When I had planned for my trek, I envisioned having FaceTime calls with Lindsay and the kids every night; however, I couldn't make time for the calls with my current schedule. The best time for a video call was around 7:00 p.m., and at that time I was usually rushing towards my camping destination for the night.

By mid-afternoon, I had made it to the Silver Creek Conservation Area, the section of the trail that is a 30-minute run from my home. I took a selfie in front of the trailhead for the Great Esker Side Trail, one of my favourite running trails, and it felt like I was seeing an old friend. I began filling my water from rivers and streams now that I was north of Georgetown, and this marked an important transition point of my journey since I no longer needed to rely on water caches. I felt more comfortable filtering water now that I had hiked past most of the large cities on the Bruce Trail. I had brought two filter flasks with me: a one-litre and a 500-millilitre silicone flask. My filter flask setup was simple: the filters were built into each of the flask caps and I squeezed water through the filter caps every time I took a drink.

I continued to pass through some of my favourite local sections of trail, including the Cheltenham Badlands, an area north of the large city of

Brampton. The Badlands are known for their view of a wide stretch of rolling hills that have the striking colour of rusty red and orange. I got some inquisitive looks from tourists as I passed through the area, I believe due to my pungent smell. I'd had a lot of time to reflect on my stench during my long hours alone, and earlier in the day I had pinpointed what I smelled like—cow manure. There was hope for me though. I could have a shower when I reached the Forks of the Credit Inn.

I carried on despite feeling self-conscious of my odour and finally made my way to the steep section of escarpment called Devil's Pulpit, right outside of Forks of the Credit Provincial Park. The sun had set by that point and I was concerned about descending the treacherous section of trail in the dark. I had navigated these steep and rocky trails at night on a previous occasion, though, and that experience gave me the confidence to start my descent. Taking it slow, I made sure of my footing as I descended the steep set of stairs at the top of the cliff. I was glad to have my trekking poles and I used them to stabilize myself as I continued down the escarpment. After 30 minutes of slow progress, I had made it down Devil's Pulpit and into the small town of Belfountain, just outside of the Forks of the Credit Park.

It was 9:00 p.m. and I still had another hour to go before I reached the Forks of the Credit Inn. I wanted nothing more than to have dinner and set up camp, but I needed to keep going so I could pick up my supply box. I got a FaceTime call from Lindsay and the kids as I was walking through Belfountain, and I took the call as I was standing on the side of the main street. My family was glad to see me; although, they were put off that I was in complete darkness. I needed to take off my headlamp and shine it on my face so that Lindsay and the kids could see me. I could sense that my family was worried about me, though they all put on brave faces and encouraged me to keep going. I felt better about my situation after my call and I set off with renewed determination, summoning the energy to run at a good pace through the Forks of the Credit Park.

An hour later, I finally arrived at the Forks of the Credit Inn. I had been emailing the manager over the last few days and had worked out that I would stay in a small outdoor cabin that they called the bunkie. The manager had stored a key for me in a combination lockbox that was left on the door handle. I felt a great sense of relief when I entered the cabin and saw my supply box and an electric kettle. With use of the kettle, I wouldn't have to use my butane stove to boil water for my meals.

After dropping my backpack, I opened my supply box and immediately went for the canned pineapple. I slurped the juice, drinking it straight from the can and uttering, "oh, yeah." I had packed a big bag of chips and a chocolate bar but I was much more interested in the fruit since I had hardly eaten any fruit or vegetables over the last five days. Next, I made the short walk to the outdoor shower because it was the only water source for the bunkie.

There was an outdoor garden hose leading to a propane heater and finally to a shower head over top of a concrete platform that had a shower curtain around it. Try as I might, I couldn't figure out how to turn the shower on. Frustrated and desperate for water, I decided to send a text message to the manager even though it was close to 11:00 p.m. Despite the hour, I received a prompt text message back explaining that I needed to push a button on the shower head to make it work. I went back outside and pressed on the shower-head button as hard as I could. I had tried the button earlier but it had been stuck and wouldn't depress. To my great joy, the button depressed this time and water flowed from the shower head. After waiting a few minutes for the water to warm up, I stepped under the warm stream of water fully clothed and enjoyed the familiar and comforting feeling. I got to work washing myself and each piece of clothing with the small bar of soap that I had packed, and I put special emphasis on washing my one and only pair of quick-dry underwear. As a final step, I filled my hydration bladder with water and went back inside to make my dinner. I felt much more human that night as I went to sleep on a plush mattress with sheets and a comforter. That being said, I didn't get to bed until midnight since I needed to spend time tending to my feet. I would pay the price for the late night the next morning.

***

I woke up at 5:30 a.m. the next morning feeling tired, but I didn't dwell on it since I needed to pack my supplies and get back on the trail. Despite my rush, I relished the use of the electric kettle when preparing my breakfast. After brewing and drinking my regular cup of coffee, I made another cup of coffee from the already used grinds. As to be expected, the second cup of coffee was weak but I still enjoyed the luxury of multiple cups of coffee in the morning. As I was packing up to leave, I was dismayed that my battery pack hadn't charged even though I had plugged it in the night before. I relied on this small battery pack to charge my phone and my GPS tracker while I was on the trail. The bunkie's electrical system must not have supported the type of current that my battery pack needed. I had another three days to hike before I reached my next supply box, where I had another charged battery pack waiting. I was worried that my phone and GPS tracker would die before I reached my supply box; however, I couldn't do anything about it, so I continued with my preparations and left the bunkie shortly after sunrise.

I set off on the roughly two-and-a-half kilometre side trail I had followed from the main trail the previous night to get to the Forks of the Credit Inn. Making good time, I crossed a very familiar-looking trail intersection but I didn't pay this any mind until I crossed the same intersection again 10 minutes later. Holding my head in frustration, I realized that I was going in circles. The lack of sleep and the 70 kilometres that I had travelled the previous day had worn me down and I wasn't as sharp as usual. I was also feeling the effects of limited downtime and the constant pressure to push my pace. My only extended rest period during any given day was to sleep, since I spent most of my downtime tending to my feet. Swearing under my breath, I pulled up Google Maps on my phone and monitored my progress as I moved closer to the main Bruce Trail. With the help of my phone, I finally got back on the main trail but I had burned half an hour on my detour.

Despite my slow start, I made good time that morning since the trail was made up of long stretches of dirt road. I had covered around 18 kilometres in four hours when I got on Airport Road, around 30 kilometres north of Brampton. Airport Road is often used by Greater Toronto Area residents to get to Collingwood and Muskoka, two popular areas for cottaging. The road was particularly busy since it was a Friday, and I feared for my life while walking on the shoulder of the road as cars zoomed by at speeds of over 100 kilometres per hour. Fortunately, I made it through the two kilometers on Airport Road without getting creamed by a car. I wasn't done with busy roads for the day, however, having more dangerous road kilometres ahead of me.

At that point, I had become acutely aware of a significant pain in my left knee. I knew that I had aggravated my IT band and that the strain was likely due to all the flat hiking and running I had been doing on the long stretches of road. I gritted my teeth and continued making progress through Mono Mills, the small town that was my final destination on my dry-run hike two months earlier. After an hour of painful progress, I decided to send Ray Zahab a text message since Ray had offered his help before I left. I got a call from Ray shortly after my text and we talked through my issue. Ray asked if I had been stretching and I explained that I stretched every night, though I could probably spend more time on it. He also asked if I had ibuprofen and I explained that I had only brought Tylenol. Ray mentioned that not bringing ibuprofen was a big miss since Tylenol was a pain reliever instead of an anti-inflammatory. In the end, Ray recommended that I continue to stretch and that I should stay off my left side when I went to sleep that night. I didn't think the way I slept had anything to do with my IT band; however, I was going to follow Ray's advice since he had so much expedition experience. I ended our phone call with a smile on my face, reflecting on Ray's parting piece of advice, which was "don't be a flower." Ray was joking, of course, yet there was a good amount of truth in his statement. I had a lot of experience with aggravating my IT band and I knew that this strain wasn't going to cripple me. Although I was still in pain, I was energized by my conversation since Ray was so positive and energetic.

I continued at a good pace through the Caledon Hills section and enjoyed the expansive views of the countryside. Fortunately, I got a break from the road hiking and enjoyed covering roughly 15 kilometres of forested trail. My IT band benefited from the change of terrain and the pain subsided significantly as it grew later in the day.

At 8:30 p.m., I emerged onto another stretch of road just outside of a tourist area called Hockley Valley. Located around 40 kilometres to the northwest of Brampton, the resort in Hockley Valley is a popular weekend destination for Greater Toronto Area residents. Once again, I had a sinking feeling as I ran on the shoulder of Highway 7, one of the busier back-road highways. I decided to travel against traffic since I was wearing my headlamp and I felt like I would be more visible to cars travelling towards me. Although the cars frightened me as they sped past, I'm sure that I scared the drivers in turn since they wouldn't expect to see a hiker on the side of a busy highway at night. I spent a nail-biting 15 minutes running on Highway 7 and was relieved to see signs for the Hockley Valley Provincial Nature Reserve. I spotted another person who was wearing a headlamp as I approached the Nature Reserve and I called, "Hello" as I approached. With my limited visibility, I noticed a young man who was rummaging in his large backpack and who was accompanied by his dog. As I came within 10 metres, I asked the backpacker if he was hiking the trail and got a muttered response back.

"Shining your headlamp in my face . . . You're so fucking rude . . . "

Naturally, I wasn't sure if I had heard him correctly so I called out again, asking if everything was okay. This time, I was sure of what I heard through.

"You're so fucking rude."

"If you don't want to chat, that's okay, I'll just keep going," I said.

The backpacker didn't say anything at all this time and turned his back to me. I was dumbfounded at how I had offended the backpacker but I was more than relieved to leave him behind as I got onto forested trail. By that point, it was 9:00 p.m. and I had planned on setting up camp as soon as I found a suitable site. I was spooked by my encounter with the backpacker, though, and decided that I needed to put some distance between the two of us. Motivated by my uneasiness, I hiked and ran at a good pace for another half hour before setting up camp. Although I didn't want to scare Lindsay, I thought it was prudent to let her know about my strange encounter and I asked her to take special note of my camping location that night. Lindsay was following my progress online through my GPS tracker. I paid extra attention to the sounds in the woods as I finally drifted off to sleep that night.

Waking up the next morning, I was dismayed to see that I had completely drained my battery pack while charging my phone and GPS tracker overnight. My phone had been my lifeline during my trek since I listened to music and audiobooks for long stretches during the day and also had lengthy phone calls with Lindsay. I had a full charge on my phone, though, and was getting closer to my next supply box, which was 130 kilometres away in the town of Collingwood. I had travelled around 60 kilometres the previous day and thought that I could cover 65 kilometres during each of the next two days so that I could reach my supply box in time to charge my devices. I was also happy that Ray's advice had worked and the pain from my IT band felt more manageable since I had stayed off my left side during the night. My feet had become very painful, though, and I made slow progress during the first few hours of the day. There were the ever-present blisters on my feet, which I drained every night and taped every morning, in addition to general soreness. Up to that point, I had only been taking Tylenol before bed since it helped me sleep; however, I resolved to take Tylenol at breakfast, lunch, and before bed that day to help me deal with the pain.

Fortunately, the pain subsided significantly by mid-morning and I was able to run at a decent pace through Mono Cliffs Provincial Park. True to its name, the park has cliffs on the escarpment that offer stunning views of blue skies and fields of dark evergreen trees that stretch to the horizon. As noon drew closer, I suffered from a wave of intense fatigue and decided that I would lie down on the side of the trail for a five-minute nap. I pulled the brim of my ball cap over my eyes and rested my head on my backpack. I fell asleep as soon as I closed my eyes and woke up with a start to the sound of my watch alarm five minutes later. I felt surprisingly refreshed from my short rest.

I got back on my way, hiking through Boyne Valley Provincial Park where I got another beautiful view of the countryside. I was still listening to audiobooks and music on my phone freely despite my concern about battery life. This decision would come back to bite me in a big way the next day, though I wasn't concerned at the moment. I made steady progress in the afternoon but the pain in my feet and left knee returned as it grew later in the day. My feet were killing me by the time I made it to a small town called Kilgorie at around 7:00 p.m. Hiking slowly on my tender feet, I passed an abandoned power mill that had decrepit grey walls and was missing windows. The roof was gone completely and plants and trees grew right through the floor. I normally enjoy coming across this sort of ruin; however, I felt uneasy since I was secluded in the woods and it was getting dark. I didn't linger or take any photos and continued making progress.

As the sun went down, so did my mood and I felt a great amount of despair. I reflected on my overall progress of roughly 440 kilometres, which was nearly the halfway point. Over the last two days, I had begrudgingly accepted that my original plan of completing the Bruce Trail in 13 days was out of reach. I would get to the halfway point at the end of the next day, day 8, which meant that I would have at least another eight full days on the trail. This meant that I would need to call my manager and ask for another two days off work, which was a distressing thought. Having an A-type personality, I'm very concerned with my perceived effort at work and I didn't want my manager or colleagues questioning my dedication. I realize now that asking for an extra two days off wouldn't have been a big deal, but it was difficult for me to find perspective at that time.

Feeling discouraged, I made camp early that night in a forested area just outside of Kilgorie. I finished setting up my tent around 8:00 p.m. and noted that I had only completed 60 of the 65 kilometres that I needed. Oh well, I thought, I would make up the extra five kilometres the next day. I simply couldn't push it any further. Despite my exhaustion, I found the energy to tend to my feet and then fell asleep a short time later to the sound of fireworks. It was Labour Day weekend and the residents of Kilgorie were celebrating.

Waking up at 4:30 a.m. the next morning, I didn't feel renewed like I hoped I would. My feet and left knee had become more painful overnight and I hobbled around as I broke camp. I had no idea how I was going to cover the 70 kilometres to my supply box in The Blue Mountains. To make matters worse, I had only around 20 percent of battery life left on my phone and GPS tracker. I would need to carefully conserve power, which meant I couldn't listen to music or audiobooks and I could only have short phone calls with Lindsay. I carried on despite these mounting challenges and made slow progress. Alone in the dark woods, I imagined calling Lindsay and asking her to pick me up; I was only an hour's drive away from our home after all. I rehearsed what I would say to Lindsay in my head, going over all the reasons why I needed to quit. Thankfully, the sunrise snapped me out of my funk and I regained some optimism.

The rhythmic sound of my hiking poles striking the ground soothed me as the sun brightened the trail and my surroundings. Before my trek, I had known that lack of sunlight affected my mood, but this trip made me realize just how sensitive I am to sunlight. The Tylenol, sunlight, and the movement of my body were the elixirs that I needed, and I managed to hit my regular pace of roughly five kilometres per hour as the morning progressed.

I crossed the Noisy River on a 20-metre-long wooden bridge at around 2:30 p.m. I was in Noisy River Provincial Park, which is a short drive west of a small town called Creemore, known for its namesake craft beer. The clear emerald water of the Noisy River gurgled along as I stepped off the bridge, and I thought about how I didn't find the river overly noisy. I did some mental math and was discouraged when I realized that I would need to hike until 2:00 a.m. to reach my supply box in The Blue Mountains. I knew I couldn't last that long on the trail and I would need to make alternate plans.

I had a quick phone call with Lindsay as I hiked and she told me that she was going to call some local restaurants to see if they would deliver food for me to the trail. I only had around 1,000 calories worth of food left and I was used to fueling with at least 3,000 calories per day. I got a text message from

Lindsay an hour later with a suggestion for a restaurant outside of a ski area called Devil's Glen, around 25 kilometres away. She had spoken with the owner who had said that they might be able to help. Feeling hopeful, I set off and pushed the pace, driven by thoughts of a take-out meal.

I was expecting to hit my target pace of 5 kilometres per hour but I was slowed by technical terrain as I hiked towards Devil's Glen. Dismayed by my slow pace, I reached a trailhead at a side road at around 6:30 p.m. I was still 15 kilometres away from Devil's Glen. I decided to call the restaurant to see if I could arrange for a delivery to the trail before sunset. The owner was very polite on our call, though I could hear a slight edge to his voice as he explained that he was very busy. The dull roar of voices in the background supported his statement. I asked if someone could bring me some food and he explained that he couldn't spare any staff to help me. I was disappointed but I understood since Sunday night is one of the busiest nights of the week for a restaurant. I then used my precious phone power to call two local pizza places and asked if they could deliver to the trail. Both restaurants told me I was outside of their delivery radius and I was disappointed once again.

Having exhausted all my options for food delivery, I continued along the trail as the sun started its descent towards the horizon. I had to turn on my headlamp as I entered a dark stretch of trail that ran alongside a small river. As the sun disappeared, the throbbing pain in my feet and left knee returned with a vengeance and all the obstacles that I was facing formed a looming shadow in my mind. I still had another 45 kilometers to go to reach my supply box and I would need to get there on the dregs of any food that I had left. To make matters worse, I was almost out of battery power. My first reaction was to do what I have always done—run. I ran frantically trying to make up the time. I tried to hang on to the hope that I would complete this FKT, but something snapped in my mind and I began to cry. I knew that I was in significant emotional distress since I could count on my hand the number of times I have cried over the last 10 years.

I somehow gathered my composure so that I could call Lindsay and I pretended that everything was okay in the first few minutes of our conversation. I couldn't hold it together very long, though, and I broke down crying again as we talked about my predicament. Lindsay encouraged me to keep going, reminding me how far I had travelled already and reassuring me that things would get better. My conversation with Lindsay soothed me and I felt better as we ended our call of around 10 minutes. When the tears returned half an hour later, I called Lindsay again and let her know that I was almost convinced I needed to quit. I would make camp for the night just outside of the Nottawasaga Lookout Provincial Nature Reserve and I would see how I felt in the morning. I asked her to keep her phone near her bed so I could call her early in the morning if I needed to get picked up.

I still washed my feet and drained blisters before bed that night and I set my alarm for 6:30 a.m., giving myself two extra hours of sleep. I slept well despite the emotional turmoil that I experienced before bed. Even though I had agreed with Lindsay that I wouldn't decide about giving up until the morning, I had already let go in my mind and this decision allowed me to sleep without feeling the constant pressure to keep pushing.

Waking up to my alarm in the morning, I solidified my resignation and called Lindsay to ask her to pick me up. I broke camp while I waited and put on every piece of clothing that I had with me to keep warm. It was a brisk and rainy morning with temperatures of 8°C and I couldn't rely on my body heat to warm me up since I was sitting still. After shivering for 20 minutes, I wrapped myself in my sleeping bag, which finally warmed me up. It wasn't long before I saw our familiar SUV pull up to the trailhead, and Lindsay had a warm smile for me as I made eye contact with her. I hobbled to the trunk of our car so I could load in my filthy gear and I saw the smiling faces of our three kids who greeted me with "Daddy!" Finally, I got in to the passenger seat in the front of the car, and Lindsay placed her hand on mine and then passed me a hot coffee she had picked up. Although disappointment weighed heavily on my mind, I felt a huge sense of relief that I didn't need to battle my way out of my predicament on the trail. After eight full days and eight full nights away, I was sitting in a comfortable, warm car in the company of the people I loved the most in the world.

Ultraliving Lessons

Know Thyself

From Greek philosophers to the modern-day workplace personality tests, humans have known the benefits of self-awareness for ages. I've done a lot of self-reflection over the years and feel that I am self-aware; however, my Bruce

Trail trek uncovered personality traits that were previously hidden to me. In addition to my physical journey on the trail, I also underwent a spiritual journey.

One of the hardest parts of my trek was the lack of quality human interaction, especially with loved ones. Out of all the comforts from home I missed while on the trail, being present among my family was at the top of my list. I missed the small daily interactions with my wife and kids around our home—smiling at my family as I pass them in the hallways and hearing snippets of their conversations during the day. I realize now that I draw a great amount of strength from my family's support and that I would have been more likely to succeed in my FKT attempt if I had my family with me.

In the same summer as my Bruce Trail FKT attempt, professional ultrarunner Timothy Olson attempted to break the supported FKT for the Pacific Crest Trail (PCT), starting his attempt on June 1st. At 4,268 kilometres in length, the PCT runs along the entire west coast of the United States, starting at the Mexico border and finishing at the Canadian border. Olson had the formidable task of besting the standing FKT of 52 days, 8 hours, 25 minutes set by Karel Sabbe in 2016. I followed Olson's FKT attempt on social media, and I really connected with his updates as he would often mention his family. Olson's wife and two small boys were travelling with him in a recreational vehicle and Olson could see his family at the end of his long days of running. Olson shared this caption in his July 10th Instagram post, after he had been on the trail for 40 days.

"I'm always running back to my family. They're my everything and the strength and inspiration that keeps me going. My biggest days have been all about pushing through so I can get back "home" to them." (Olson 2021)

On July 22, 2021, Timothy Olson set a new FKT for the PCT with a total time of 51 days, 6 hours, 55 minutes.

Like Timothy Olson, I'm convinced that my relationship with my family gives me the strength to tackle life's challenges. I believe that I could have kept going on my Bruce Trail FKT attempt if I had my family with me. As such, I'm planning on leveraging the strength that I get from my family on my next FKT attempt.

It makes sense that I would uncover important information about myself by being pushed to my breaking point. Although I felt terrible when I gave up on my FKT attempt, the days of suffering allowed me to have a spiritual journey and to make important personal discoveries.

Afterward

I'm sitting at my dining room table with a steaming cup of coffee in front of me—it's early in the morning and I'm looking out the window at a blanket of fresh snow. I've had a few months to sort out my feelings about my trek and it is now early December 2021. There's no dancing around it: my Bruce Trail FKT attempt was a failure and it's clear to me now that I wasn't ready for two weeks of rugged trails.

I slept long hours when I first got back from the Bruce Trail and when I was awake, I couldn't shake feelings of fatigue and sadness. I still had a week left before I returned to work and I considered working on some projects around the house. Whenever I started a project, though, I couldn't maintain a prolonged effort. I suppose my brain needed to recover from the long days of intense focus on the trail. I turned to my journal a few days after I got home and jotted down some potential reasons why I was feeling so melancholic. I was sleep deprived from only getting five to six hours of sleep per night for the last eight nights. I felt the effects of malnourishment, as well, since I'd hardly eaten any fresh vegetables or fruit. I also didn't get the calories that I needed to support my massive effort on the trail every day. Finally, I felt the effects of adventure letdown. It was tough to return to my regular routine after so much excitement on the trail.

I relied heavily on my journal and on conversations with Lindsay during the first few weeks after my trek, and I gradually started to feel more normal. At that time, I couldn't fathom another Bruce Trail FKT attempt; however, now that a few months have gone by, I find myself longing for my experience on the Bruce Trail. I guess that is an Ultraliving Lesson in itself. After some time has passed, I have viewed all my ultrarunning experiences with fondness. The misery that I sometimes felt during an event was only transient and provided me with important opportunities for learning and progress in my ultraliving journey.

I didn't return from the Bruce Trail empty handed, even though I failed to achieve a self-supported FKT. Rather than feeling defeated, I came back with a quiet confidence from having hiked a total of 490 kilometres, an average of 60 kilometres per day for eight days, all while wearing a 30-pound backpack. I know that this act of endurance was a culmination of all my running experiences and I'm proud of what I accomplished. I'm sure that the 280 pound kid from grade 10 would be proud to know that he had this adventure in his future.

The Ultraliving Lesson of *Never Give Up* has taken on even more significance for me since I've returned from my FKT attempt. It is likely that I'll make another bid at a significant FKT in the next few years. Who knows, I might give the Bruce Trail FKT another try. Although this is a monumental challenge, I have my family and friends, and my Ultraliving Lessons, to rely on.

With Norah and James at the finish of La Sauvage in Pralognan-la-Vanoise, France in August 2015.

With Joe (left) and Chris (right) at the finish of the Sulphur Springs 100 mile race in May 2018.

Partway through the Quebec Mega Trail 110 km race in June 2019.

From left to right, Lindsay, Norah, me, David and James at the Midnight Moose 100 mile race in September, 2019.

Running with Chris (right) at the Stride Inside, 6 hour track race. [Photo by Sue Sitki, January 2020]

At the southern terminus of the Bruce Trail in August 2021.

Part Two: The Ultraliving Manual

The Ultraliving Manual

Preparing for an ultramarathon is a daunting task. Unlike the traditional running distances that take a few hours to complete, an ultramarathon can take over 30 hours of straight running. I didn't have all the answers when I first started running ultramarathons, but I worked hard over the years to figure out the right gear, the best way to train, optimal strategies for racing, and the right way to eat.

The Ultraliving Manual takes the guesswork out of ultramarathon preparation by sharing all the knowledge that I've gained through my ultrarunning journey. As demonstrated in the Ultraliving Lessons, I carefully documented all my ultrarunning experiences over the last six years and have included this knowledge in the Ultraliving Manual. Although some trial and error is inevitable as an ultrarunner, this manual will put readers on the fast track for the successful completion of their first ultramarathon and for longevity in ultrarunning.

This manual is divided into the following sections: Running Gear, Ultramarathon Training, Ultramarathon Training Plans, Ultramarathon Racing, Nutrition and Health, and Inspiration.

Running Gear, Ultramarathon Training, Ultramarathon Training Plans, and Ultramarathon Racing are all critical reading for preparing to run ultradistances. With self-explanatory titles, these sections outline all the steps necessary for a successful first ultramarathon.

The Nutrition and Health section describes my current eating and wellness practices. This material will help runners to build and maintain the health and strength needed to continue running ultramarathons over the years. The Inspiration section has a list of the top ultrarunning influencers, from the stars like Scott Jurek and Kilian Jornet, to the well-known Canadian ultrarunner Gary Robbins.

While the Ultraliving Lessons share my stories about ultrarunning, the Ultraliving Manual provides a step-by-step guide on how to run your first ultramarathon and how to continue running ultramarathons in a safe and sustainable manner. My hope is that the practical advice and inspirational material will give you a strong foundation to start your own ultraliving journey.

Running Gear

When I run with friends, our conversations often turn to our trail running gear. I'm always interested in hearing about a friend's choice of shoes, running vest and even running hat. Gear selection is particularly important for ultrarunning because of how long the races last. Defective equipment is very disruptive when you are running a 24 hour race. In this chapter, I discuss the fundamental ultrarunning gear and offer advice on how to select the best equipment.

Shoes

Starting to run on trails is not complicated; all you need is a pair of shoes. Some runners even run barefoot, which is not the best option for Canadian winters. It's important to have a good trail shoe to keep you safe and stable on the trails. I evaluate trail running shoes based on their outsoles, the body of the shoe, and their weight.

Outsoles

Trail shoes have a more aggressive tread on the outsole compared to regular running shoes. The individual grips on the outsoles are called lugs. Longer lugs help with softer surfaces like mud and snow, while shorter lugs help with hard surfaces like hard-packed dirt trails or gravel.

Many ultrarunners run in HOKA shoes, which have a very large amount of cushioning in the outsoles. HOKA's philosophy is that you need extra cushioning for the long hours of an ultramarathon. There is another school of thought that suggests you should run with the least amount of cushioning possible. As mentioned, some runners even run barefoot. Barefoot running is explored in-depth in Christopher McDougall's amazing book *Born to Run*. I have run for years, with good results in a shoe with medium cushioning, between 20 – 30 mm under the heel.

Foot protection is also very important when considering the outsole of a trail shoe. Trail shoes with stiffer outsoles or rock plates (hard plastic above the outsoles) are better suited for running rocky terrain. Shoes with softer outsoles are more suited for less technical trails where you won't be running over hard edges.

Body of the Shoe

I evaluate the body of a trail shoe by its resistance to wear, how fast it dries, and the size of its toe box. Trail shoes should be reinforced at the common wear points: the heel collar, the toe articulation point, and the toe cap. Good trail shoes should stand up to tough conditions of trail running and last for at least four months of heavy running.

Getting shoes wet is very common while trail running and it's important that trail shoes drain well and dry quickly. Running with wet shoes softens the skin on your feet and leads to blisters. Generally, the more mesh on a shoe, the faster the shoe will dry. Mesh, however, is weak material and can lead to a shoe wearing out more quickly. When evaluating a shoe, I look for a good balance of mesh and durability. I'll also rely on online reviews and shoe-store staff for opinions on how well a shoe drains water.

Finally, I recommend paying special attention to the size of a shoe's toe box. My toes are frequently pushed to the front of my shoe during ultramarathons due to downhill running and to my feet swelling. Too small of a toe box can easily lead to painful blisters and lost toenails.

Weight of the Shoe

Shoe weight is an important consideration, especially for the 100-mile distance. "A pound on your feet equals five pounds on your back" is a common saying among serious hikers. Jorgen Johansson, author of the book *Smarter Backpacking*, published an excellent blog article on the literature that backs up the advantages of taking weight off your feet for hiking. Johansson quotes two scientific studies conducted by the US Army in the 1980s that demonstrate that hiking in running shoes requires roughly five times less energy than hiking in boots (Johansson 2019). A heavier shoe can be beneficial when running technical terrain. A weighty feature like a rock plate will give your feet more protection from sharp and jagged rocks. In general, the more protection the shoe has, the heavier the shoe.

Winter Running

I do most of my winter running in my regular trail shoes with a medium thickness sock. Many runners will wear traction devices on the soles of their shoes for icy conditions. Some runners will even put small screws directly into their outsoles. While I have used traction devices, I prefer running without them since they feel awkward and change my running gait. I've found that I can run most of the winter relying on my trail shoe for traction in the snow and moderately icy conditions.

Resources

Outdoor sporting stores and running stores are great resources for finding the right trail shoe. I've relied on the staff at these stores for guidance and expertise when buying shoes. I also research trail shoes online and I'm partial to the *Ginger Runner LIVE* YouTube reviews. Ethan Newberry, the Ginger Runner, has been reviewing trail shoes for over 10 years.

Expect some trial and error before finding the right trail shoe. I went through three different shoes before finding the right one. I am now running in my fifth pair of the same model of shoe.

Hydration Packs

Next to shoes, a hydration pack is the most important piece of equipment for ultrarunners. In addition to carrying water, these packs also carry essentials like food, electrolytes, and a phone.

Water Capacity and Storage

Most trail runners use hydration packs that have two collapsible silicone water flasks that are carried on the front of the pack. These flasks are easy to access for both drinking and refilling during races. Carrying two 500-millilitre flasks will meet a runner's water needs for most trail races since ultramarathons generally have aid stations after every 10 kilometres. In very hot conditions, I like to carry a hydration bladder in the main compartment of my pack in addition to my two water flasks.

Hydration packs come in a variety of sizes for storage capacity. Most packs have stretchy pockets beneath the water flask compartments that are great for storing gels and other foods, electrolytes, and a phone. Additional storage is typically found in a pack's main compartment, which is carried on a runner's upper back. Choosing the right amount of storage capacity is dependent on the type of race. Ultramarathons in challenging environments like the mountains often require racers to carry mandatory gear, like a rain shell, emergency blanket, and headlamp. In contrast, ultrarunners are not required to have any mandatory gear for trail races in gentler environments that have regular aid stations for resupplying.

Fit

Fit is very important since you wear your pack for such a long time during an ultramarathon. Most brands have different styles of packs for women and men that are specifically designed to fit the different upper body shapes. I like my packs to fit snugly while still feeling comfortable. It's difficult to know if you have the right fit without testing the pack on a long run. I borrowed my friend's pack and used it for a three-hour training run before buying my own pack. If you can't borrow a pack from a friend, I'd suggest trying some on at a local running store.

Clothes

As funny as it sounds, managing chafing is a very important part of ultrarunning. Ill-fitting clothes can cause a lot of damage to your body in the long hours that it takes to complete an ultramarathon. I make sure to test all my running clothes before wearing them in a race. I wear my full race kit, including T-shirt, shorts, hydration pack, headlamp, hat, and shoes, for at least three long training runs to ensure that everything is in working order.

Shorts and T-Shirts

I do most of my running in quick-dry T-shirts and shorts. My only criteria when selecting a T-shirt is that it fits comfortably and that it doesn't rub my armpits or upper arms. Like T-shirts, shorts should fit comfortably without being overly tight in any spot. I pay close attention to the waistband. I like it tight, yet not so tight that it chafes. I prefer shorts that cover up to my mid-thigh as they keep my upper thighs from rubbing together.

Underwear and Sports Bras

Managing chafing down south during a race is extremely important since this type of chafing is very painful. I run in synthetic compression underwear with a longer leg to keep my thighs from rubbing together. I always make sure to test my underwear by wearing them on a long run prior to a race. For men and women, I recommend selecting snug fitting, quick-dry underwear that is specific for sport.

While I don't have first-hand experience wearing a sports bra, I can easily recognize the importance of this piece of equipment for female ultrarunners. Women will want to select a sports bra carefully to avoid chafing and excessive movement during an ultramarathon. My wife, Lindsay, recommends spending extra time on figuring out the right bra size since she has had some bad experiences running in ill-fitting sports bras. It wasn't until Lindsay visited a boutique that she realized she had been buying the wrong bra size for quite some time. As an alternative to a boutique, which can be pricy, online tools can be helpful for sizing.

Many of the top outdoor brands make running-specific underwear and sports bras. A quick internet search on underwear or sports bras for ultrarunners will bring up several strong options.

Socks

The running sock is often overlooked as the important piece of gear that it is. Improper running socks can easily cause foot damage, including blisters and lost toenails. The golden rule for a good running sock is to avoid anything made from cotton. Merino wool and synthetic blends like nylon, polyester, and spandex are far superior to cotton. I have worn a synthetic-blend running sock for the last four years with good results. My socks dry quickly, and compression in the midfoot keeps my running socks from bunching. I recommend wearing a mid-ankle height of sock to avoid scrapes and irritation from the trail.

Calf Compression Sleeves

Calf compression sleeves (calf sleeves) are tight-fitting tubes of fabric that cover your calf from just above the ankle to below your knee. Benefits of a calf sleeve include protecting your legs from irritation and preventing swelling. I'll often develop an itchy rash when I forget to wear calf sleeves on trail runs, as the tall grass brushing against my lower legs irritates my skin. Calf sleeves have also been shown to reduce the swelling in your lower legs after long periods of time on your feet (Partsch, Winiger, and Lun 2004).

Gaiters

A gaiter is a piece of cloth that wraps around the ankle and covers the top part of your shoe. Gaiters are used to keep rocks and debris out of your shoes and are ideal for sandy and muddy terrain. Gaiters can prevent chafing and can save time in a race by reducing the number of times that you have to remove your shoes to shake out dirt and debris.

Head Gear

A meshed-back trucker hat is an integral part of the unofficial trail runner uniform for women and men alike. I prefer trucker hats made from quick-dry material and I always choose comfort over style. In addition to my trucker hat, I love wearing my buff. Very simply, a buff is a tube of stretchy, lightweight material. Buffs are versatile—I wear them as a headband, as a toque, and around my neck to block the sun or keep the bugs away. A buff filled with ice and placed on your neck is a great way to beat the heat. Buffs also store easily when not being used.

Winter Clothes

I have a hard time getting motivated to run in the winter. The darkness and the cold weather make me want to curl up under a blanket rather than bear the elements. Although it takes me more time to get out the door for my winter runs, afterwards I'm always glad that I went for a run. Winter running helps me beat cabin fever and overcome the winter blues, which is common in Canada.

Temperatures: -3°C to +5°C

As a good Canadian, I consider -3°C a very reasonable temperature for running. When running in these conditions, I typically stay warm by wearing two layers of clothes. To keep my legs warm, I wear a pair of standard running tights with my shorts over top. On my upper body I'll wear a long-sleeved quick-dry shirt with a quick-dry T-shirt over top. A buff is usually sufficient to keep my head warm. I like the versatility of a buff—I can pull the buff down and cover my ears if needed or I can adjust the buff so that it fits more like a headband. I wear thin cotton gloves, the cheap ones that you get at the grocery store, to keep my hands warm. If needed, I'll wear another thin pair of gloves over top.

Temperatures: -3°C or colder

Warm running pants are helpful in colder conditions. Winter running pants are expensive; however, they are well worth the investment. I spent $100 on running pants 10 years ago and I've been wearing them ever since. I'm always amazed by how warm I'm kept by these relatively thin and flexible pants.

I'll add a layer and wear running tights underneath my pants when it gets really cold (-20°C or colder). A word of caution for men: despite the layering, it can still get very cold on my undercarriage during long runs. I have yet to find an ideal solution for this problem; however, wearing two pairs of underwear has been helpful.

For my upper body, I wear a long-sleeved quick-dry base layer, a quick-dry sweater, and a running jacket. I'll remove the sweater and tie it around my waist if I get too hot. For head gear, I continue to wear a buff while temperatures stay above -10°C. When temperatures fall below -10°C, I switch to a synthetic toque that I can pull down over my ears. I wear a face warmer when it gets really cold, below -25°C. This is uncomfortable at first, as it feels strange having a cloth over your mouth when breathing hard, though I eventually get used to it.

Watches

We are in the golden age of running watches. Watches can do everything from playing music to tracking your stress level. I really enjoy checking all my metrics and I hardly ever take my watch off as a result.

The biggest advantage of a running watch is that it heightens your training awareness. Peter Drucker, the well-known business author, is often given credit for the famous phrase "what gets measured gets managed." Seeing your distances and health metrics improve every week is very motivating.

Most running watches allow you to connect to social media style apps which share your progress with your friends. These apps let you encourage your connections by liking or commenting on their running activities. You can also challenge your friends to step or distance contests. My brother-in-law is really motivated by step contests and we have been doing a weekly contest for over a year.

Running watches are expensive but worth the investment. I ran for two years without a good watch and I couldn't believe what I was missing when I finally bought a high-quality watch.

Watches During Races

Watches are important for timing nutrition and monitoring pace and progress while racing. During a race, I take a few sips of water every 15 minutes and take a gel and a salt pill every hour. As a result, I'm frequently glancing at my watch to ensure that I'm getting the proper nutrition. While racing, I can glance at my watch and know my running pace in real time. Although I don't obsess over pace, I like the reassurance that I'm close to my target pace during a race. Finally, knowing the distance that I have covered during a race is very reassuring, especially when a race course does not have distance markers. Towards the end of a long race, I have a small celebration in my mind every time another kilometre ticks by on my watch.

Additional Equipment

Headlamps

I've developed a special relationship with my headlamp over my years of trail running. Illuminating the unknown, my headlamp feels like a warm blanket when I'm running through the darkness in the middle of the night. Headlamps are particularly important for technical races—it's easy to trip on roots and rocks if you can't see them.

There is a fine balance between battery life and weight. Heavy headlamps can put a lot of strain on your neck during long races. Generally, the more you pay for a headlamp, the longer its battery life and the lighter it is.

Trekking Poles

Trekking poles are a terrific aid for trail running, especially for hilly terrain. Trekking poles look similar to ski poles but they are generally lighter. Also similar to ski poles, you hold one trekking pole in each hand while running. Although running with poles might seem awkward at first, the motion starts to feel natural after a little practice. My standard technique for running with poles on flat terrain is to alternate planting left and right poles every three strides. I'll plant my right pole at the same time as a left footfall and vice versa.

One of the main reasons I like to use trekking poles is that poles allow me to get my upper body more involved in trail running. I've found that using my upper body for forward propulsion gives my legs a much-needed rest during an ultramarathon.

A cautionary tale on using trekking poles: it's very important to train with poles before racing with them. A few years ago, I used poles to complete a 100-mile race without prior pole training. My arm and back muscles were okay during the race; however, they were severely strained afterwards. It took two months of focused stretching and massage therapy for my back to return to normal.

Audio

Although music and audiobooks are not necessarily gear, they play an important role in my running. I really enjoy listening to music on training runs and during races. Being out on the trail for hours can get boring and music gives me some relief. Although I listen to music freely on training runs, I am strategic with listening to music during races.

I love the beginning of an ultramarathon and I do my best to savour that part of the experience. The start of an ultramarathon is my only chance to run with a large group of people and I enjoy the communal aspect of running. I keep the music off so that I can soak in the sights, sounds, and smells. I'll turn the music on a few hours later when the excitement has dissipated.

I like to listen to audiobooks even more than music. Consuming audiobooks during a run has become one of my favourite activities and my preferred way to read books. I've finished over 75 audiobooks over the last five years.

With the fundamentals of running gear covered, we are ready to move on to ultramarathon training. The next chapter discusses all the best practices for training that I have discovered over my six years of running ultramarathons.

Ultramarathon Training

Ultramarathons are always going to be painful; however, being prepared is a surefire way to lessen the pain. In this section, I outline several of the strategies I use to ensure I am training effectively for ultramarathons. Training logistics and the types of ultramarathon training are covered in detail in this chapter, while detailed training plans are included in the following chapter.

Logistics

Distance Progression

I recommend progressing through most of the ultramarathon distances before attempting a 100 miler. Each race distance is unique and enjoyable, and building your distance ensures that you are ready for the monumental task of running 100 miles. My race progression was: 50 kilometres, 50 miles (80 kilometres), and 100 miles (160 kilometres). I had at least three months between each race and I had been running ultramarathons for three years before attempting and completing my first 100 miler.

Logging Hours Instead of Distance

I have been measuring my running in hours instead of distance for years with good results. Running for distance can be discouraging, especially at the beginning of a training program. It might take me 2 hours, 30 minutes to run 20 kilometres on trails at the start of my training block and only 2 hours, 15 minutes to run the same distance at the end of my training.

I also enjoy the flexibility in this type of training. Since I only have a time goal, I can manage the intensity of my run based on how I'm feeling. If I feel great during a training run, I'll increase the intensity and run fast. If I'm feeling tired, I'll slow down my pace and will focus on completing the training session.

That being said, I examine my statistics from my smartwatch after most runs to know the distance that I've covered. While I don't overanalyze my running pace during training, I like to know that I'll finish my upcoming ultramarathon in a reasonable amount of time. For example, from my years of training, I know that covering eight kilometres per hour on an easy trail is a good training pace. If I'm off this pace by around 20 percent or more, I know that I need to work on my speed.

Weekend Runs

Long runs are the key to ultratraining. I can miss one or two of my runs during the week and still maintain my training if I stay on track with my long runs. I do my long runs on the weekend when I don't have any work commitments. My long runs are between one-and-a-half to five hours, and I typically run in the morning so I have enough time with my family during the day. In my 100-mile training plan, I only schedule one five-hour run. Training runs that are longer than five hours can put you at a higher risk for injury and, really, who has time to run for more than five hours.

I like back-to-back long runs since they give me the benefit of running on tired legs without having to be out all day. For a 100-mile race, my training peaks with a four-hour run on Saturday followed by a five-hour run on Sunday.

Ultratraining with Kids

I have three kids, I'm married, and I have a demanding full-time job. I don't have much room in my schedule, but I always make time for running by keeping a flexible training schedule. In this section, I discuss how I balance running with childcare.

Despite my best efforts, there are weekends when I can't run early in the morning. From sports practices to play dates, there is always a lot to do when kids are involved. When this happens, I will do half of my run in the morning and the other half in the afternoon. For example, if I have a four-hour run scheduled, I'll run for two hours in the morning, come back to make lunch for my family, and then run for another two hours so that I'm back to make dinner.

When my kids were younger, I would make time for my runs by bringing my kids with me in a running stroller. Our stroller would hold two kids comfortably and even hold our family dog. The stroller was an expensive purchase; however, it was well worth the investment since we used it all the time. I would run with the stroller on easy trails and my kids enjoyed being out in nature. We would often stop at a park halfway through the run so that my kids could stretch their legs and play.

While finding time for training runs is an important part of training, getting the proper amount of rest is equally as important. This next section describes the optimal parameters for rest and tapering.

Rest and Tapering

With so many hours of running, ultratraining can take its toll on your body and mind. A runner can easily become injured or burned out without the proper amount of rest and recovery. I make sure to take a full rest day every week, during which I won't do any type of training other than stretching. Monday works well for this rest day since I do my long runs on the weekend. I also take a rest week after every two weeks of training to give my body enough time to recover. During these rest weeks, I continue with my regular runs during the week but I decrease the length of my weekend runs to one to one-and-a-half hours. I also decrease the intensity of my weight workouts by dropping one set from all exercises. For example, if I usually do three sets of 12 push-ups, I will only do two sets of 12 push-ups during my rest week.

A taper refers to a significant period of rest before your race. Putting in the hours of rest during a taper is just as important as putting in the hours of running earlier in a training plan. Tapering ensures that you are in your best shape for your race by giving your body time to fully recover from training. I usually taper for two weeks before a race; however, research has shown that runners can taper for three weeks without losing any fitness (Cooper 2021). During a taper period, I will stop weight training to allow my muscles to fully recover before a race. Recommended rest periods and taper periods are described in detail in the upcoming Ultrarunning Training Plan section.

10 Percent Rule

As shown in the next chapter, I follow three-month training plans for ultramarathons. During these three months, I steadily increase my total weekly running hours by roughly 10 percent until race weekend. These 10-percent increases, along with taking rest weeks, have helped me avoid injury and burnout during my training.

Work-Week Runs

I run four days per week during the work week and I keep these runs to one hour. With my family and work commitments, it's hard to find more than one hour per day to run. I usually run at lunch since it's a nice way to split up my day. If I can't run at lunch, I run early in the morning or in the evening.

Terrain

I had a very tough time at the 2019 Quebec Mega Trail (QMT) 110 km because the terrain was very technical with a lot of mud, roots, and rocks. I had done the proper amount of running to prepare for the race but I trained on the wrong terrain. Most of my long training runs were done on relatively easy trails that didn't resemble the terrain at QMT.

Since QMT, I make sure to thoroughly research the expected terrain at a race and I prepare accordingly. If I'm going to be racing on hilly and rocky trails, I do most of my long runs on hilly and rocky trails.

Types of Training

Speed Work

Many runners and coaches recommend incorporating at least one training session of speed work per week. The most popular forms of speed work include tempo runs, Fartleks, and intervals.

Tempo runs are done at a faster pace than a typical easy run. My tempo run consists of a five-minute warm-up at an easy pace, followed by 40 minutes of running at around 70 percent of my maximum effort or just below my 10-kilometre race pace.

As Joel H. Cohen states in his hilarious book *How to Lose a Marathon*, there is no denying that Fartlek has the word "fart" in it. In addition to getting a good giggle whenever I say the word Fartlek, this type of training is very effective for developing speed. Fartlek means "speed play" in Swedish and it involves short bursts of speed followed by easy running. My Fartlek runs consist of 10 minutes of warm-up, 20 minutes of Fartlek, and then 10 minutes of cool down. During the 20-minute Fartlek period, I run repeats of a sequence of hard for one to two minutes and then recover for one to two minutes. I maintain a pace of around 80 percent of maximum effort during the hard periods, which allows me to run at my normal easy pace during the recovery periods.

Although interval training is similar to Fartleks, intervals are done at a higher effort. Interval training typically consists of short periods of near maximum effort followed by short periods of rest where you are standing or sitting down. Interval training is better suited for the shorter running distances, since ultrarunners will rarely run at maximum effort during a race.

I'm sure that I would benefit from more speed work in my training; however, I haven't done speed work consistently for the six years that I have been running ultramarathons. Despite the lack of speed work in my training, I've significantly improved my speed during ultramarathons. While speed work is important for a more seasoned ultrarunner, I don't think beginners should focus on speed training. I believe that ultrarunners can train effectively for their first ultramarathon without doing any speed work.

Hill Training

As described earlier in the chapter, when I'm training for an ultramarathon, I run on terrain that is similar to the terrain at the race. For example, if I can expect rolling hills and a gravel trail, I do most of my training on this type of terrain. However, when I'm preparing for a mountain race, I need to incorporate hill repeats into my training. Living in Ontario, Canada, I don't have access to large mountains for training. As a result, I'll find a suitable hill and will run repeats. I usually run hill repeats during one long training session on the weekend. I'll aim to climb the same number of metres per hour that I can expect during the race. For example, if I'm preparing for a 50-kilometre race with 5,000 metres of elevation and I believe that I can complete the race in seven hours, I will aim to climb around 714 metres every hour (5,000 metres/7 hours) during my training. I always make sure to ease into hill repeats, as this type of training puts a big strain on my knees and hips. I start my hill repeat training with one hour of hill repeats during my weekend long run. At my next weekend long run, I'll increase the amount of time by 20 percent and will do this every week until I'm running hills for the entirety of one of my long runs. For example, during my one-and-a-half-hour run on week 1, I run one hour of hill repeats. On week 2, during my two-hour training run, I run 1 hour, 12 minutes of hill repeats.

Cross-Training

Cross-training with cycling, swimming, cross-country skiing, and other activities is a great way to build strength, prevent injury, and provide variety. I ride my gravel bike every week for one of my training sessions, which gives my legs a break from the repetitive motion of running. A gravel bike is like a road bike but the tires are larger with a more aggressive tread. As the name implies, I can ride on gravel roads with a gravel bike rather than having to ride smooth paved roads like I would on a traditional road bike.

Swimming is another one of my favourite cross-training sports. Swimming is a low-impact activity that helps build core muscles. Although cross-training is beneficial, it's important to remember that logging time on your feet during training runs is your top priority as an ultrarunner.

Weight Training

Weight training becomes particularly important as runners age. In the absence of lifting weights, you can lose as much as 5 percent of your muscle mass per decade after turning 30 (Harvard Health Publishing 2016). What's more, weight training helps maintain joint health. As a runner, your knee and hip joints take an incredible amount of impact. Weight training helps to bolster these joints, decreasing the likelihood of injury and the amount of wear and tear.

My weight workouts are short, at 15 to 20 minutes per session. I'll typically do weights at the end of a run since I find it difficult to work out more than once during the day. As shown in the upcoming training plan section, I'll perform each of the workouts below during the week since the weekend is typically reserved for long runs. I've seen a huge benefit to my running since I started lifting weights regularly. I am leaner, I can run hills more easily, and I experience fewer injuries.

Weight-Training Plan

Day 1: Legs
- Deadlifts: 12 reps x 3 sets
- Squats: 12 reps x 3 sets
- Lunges with dumbbells: 20 reps x 2 sets

Day 2: Core
- Planks: 30 reps x 3 sets
- Bicycle crunches: 20 reps, 15 reps, 10 reps
- Russian twists: 20 reps, 15 reps, 10 reps

Day 3: Chest and Back
- Push-ups: 20 reps, 12 reps, 8 reps
- Pull-ups: 8 reps, 6 reps, 6 reps
- Shoulder presses: 12 reps x 2 sets

Hiking

Hiking is frequently overlooked in training plans even though it is a key skill for ultrarunners. I typically spend 20 percent of my time hiking during an ultramarathon trail race. I hike most hills and take 5-to 20-minute hiking breaks when I need a rest during the later stages of a race. I train the same way that I race, hiking uphill and running downhill. Hiking isn't only for amateur runners; elite runners also hike during ultramarathons.

Training Races

Training races are a great way to stay motivated. I ran the Sulphur Springs 50 km in May 2019, one month before the Quebec Mega Trail 110 km. The race fit in nicely with my training plan and I placed a solid 15th out of 184 runners. Sulphur Springs was a great confidence booster and kept me motivated to complete the rest of my training for the Quebec Mega Trail.

Having discussed the high-level strategies of ultramarathon training, we are now ready to cover the detailed training plans for all the common ultramarathon distances.

Ultrarunning Training Plans

I've included my tested ultramarathon training plans in this chapter. A disclaimer: these plans are meant for runners who can already run a 10-kilometre training run comfortably.

These training plans do not prescribe distances, but instead they leave room for you to adjust the intensity of your training based on feel. I make sure that I feel challenged but not completely exhausted by most of my training runs. One exception is the last week or two of hard training before a race. I usually feel very tired during these last weeks; however, I use the two-week taper period before a race to recover.

When I first started running, I put a lot of pressure on myself to carry out 100 percent of my training plan. I have since realized that an effective plan guides training and leaves room for flexibility. Ultramarathon training plans take a long time to complete and it is common to get sick or develop a strain while training. If I need some extra time for recovery, I'll skip a run or will decrease the length of a long run. I've found that I can lighten my training plan in response to sickness or injury and still accomplish my running goals.

Speed work is left as optional in these training plans. As mentioned in the previous chapter, I don't believe that beginners should focus on speed work.

If you choose to do speed work, you can alternate between tempo runs and Fartleks every week. For example, you can run tempo on week 1, Fartleks on week 2, and come back to tempo on week 3.

The parameters for rest, including tapering, weights, and cross-training, are outlined in the previous chapter.

The following training plans are for the common ultramarathon distances, which include: 50 kilometres, 50 miles (80 kilometres), 100 kilometres, and 100 miles (160 kilometres).

50 km Training Plan

Month 1

	Mon	Tues	Wed	Thurs	Fri	Sat	Sun
Week 1	Rest	45 min run + 15 min weights	45 min run + 15 min weights Optional: speed work	45 min run + 15 min weights	1 hour run or cross-train	1 hour run	1.5 hour run
Week 2	Rest	45 min run + 15 min weights	45 min run + 15 min weights Optional: speed work	45 min run + 15 min weights	1 hour run or cross-train	1 hour run	2 hour run
Week 3 (Rest)	Rest	45 min run + 15 min weights	45 min run + 15 min weights Optional: speed work	45 min run + 15 min weights	1 hour run or cross-train	1 hour run	1.5 hour run
Week 4	Rest	45 min run + 15 min weights	45 min run + 15 min weights Optional: speed work	45 min run + 15 min weights	1 hour run or cross-train	1 hour run	3 hour run

Month 2

	Mon	Tues	Wed	Thurs	Fri	Sat	Sun
Week 5	Rest	45 min run + 15 min weights	45 min run + 15 min weights Optional: speed work	45 min run + 15 min weights	1 hour run or cross-train	1 hour run	3.5 hour run
Week 6 (Rest)	Rest	45 min run + 15 min weights	45 min run + 15 min weights Optional: speed work	45 min run + 15 min weights	1 hour run or cross-train	1 hour run	1.5 hour run
Week 7	Rest	45 min run + 15 min weights	45 min run + 15 min weights Optional: speed work	45 min run + 15 min weights	1 hour run or cross-train	1 hour run	4 hour run
Week 8	Rest	45 min run + 15 min weights	45 min run + 15 min weights Optional: speed work	45 min run + 15 min weights	1 hour run or cross-train	1.5 hour run	4 hour run

Month 3

	Mon	Tues	Wed	Thurs	Fri	Sat	Sun
Week 9 (Rest)	Rest	45 min run + 15 min weights	45 min run + 15 min weights Optional: speed work	45 min run + 15 min weights	1 hour run or cross-train	1 hour run	1.5 hour run
Week 10	Rest	45 min run + 15 min weights	45 min run + 15 min weights Optional: speed work	45 min run + 15 min weights	1 hour run or cross-train	2 hour run	4 hour run
Week 11	Rest	45 min run + 15 min weights	45 min run + 15 min weights Optional: speed work	45 min run + 15 min weights	1 hour run or cross-train	2.5 hour run	4 hour run
Week 12 (Taper)	Rest	1 hour run	1 hour run	1 hour run	1 hour run or cross-train	1 hour run	1 hour run
Week 13 (Taper)	Rest	30 min run or walk	30 min run or walk	30 min walk	Rest or 30 min walk	**50 km Race**	

50-Mile/100 km Training Plan

Month 1

	Mon	Tues	Wed	Thurs	Fri	Sat	Sun
Week 1	Rest	45 min run + 15 min weights	45 min run + 15 min weights Optional: speed work	45 min run + 15 min weights	1 hour run or cross-train	1 hour run	2.5 hour run
Week 2	Rest	45 min run + 15 min weights	45 min run + 15 min weights Optional: speed work	45 min run + 15 min weights	1 hour run or cross-train	1 hour run	3 hour run
Week 3 (Rest)	Rest	45 min run + 15 min weights	45 min run + 15 min weights Optional: speed work	45 min run + 15 min weights	1 hour run or cross-train	1 hour run	1.5 hour run
Week 4	Rest	45 min run + 15 min weights	45 min run + 15 min weights Optional: speed work	45 min run + 15 min weights	1 hour run or cross-train	2 hour run	3 hour run

Month 2

	Mon	Tues	Wed	Thurs	Fri	Sat	Sun
Week 5	Rest	45 min run + 15 min weights	45 min run + 15 min weights Optional: speed work	45 min run + 15 min weights	1 hour run or cross-train	2 hour run	3.5 hour run
Week 6 (Rest)	Rest	45 min run + 15 min weights	45 min run + 15 min weights Optional: speed work	45 min run + 15 min weights	1 hour run or cross-train	1 hour run	1.5 hour run
Week 7	Rest	45 min run + 15 min weights	45 min run + 15 min weights Optional: speed work	45 min run + 15 min weights	1 hour run or cross-train	2 hour run	4 hour run
Week 8	Rest	45 min run + 15 min weights	45 min run + 15 min weights Optional: speed work	45 min run + 15 min weights	1 hour run or cross-train	2.5 hour run	4 hour run

Month 3

	Mon	Tues	Wed	Thurs	Fri	Sat	Sun
Week 9 (Rest)	Rest	45 min run + 15 min weights	45 min run + 15 min weights Optional: speed work	45 min run + 15 min weights	1 hour run or cross-train	1 hour run	1.5 hour run
Week 10	Rest	45 min run + 15 min weights	45 min run + 15 min weights Optional: speed work	45 min run + 15 min weights	1 hour run or cross-train	3.5 hour run	4 hour run
Week 11	Rest	45 min run + 15 min weights	45 min run + 15 min weights Optional: speed work	45 min run + 15 min weights	1 hour run or cross-train	4 hour run	4 hour run
Week 12 (Taper)	Rest	1 hour run	1 hour run	1 hour run	1 hour run or cross-train	1 hour run	1.5 hour run
Week 13 (Taper)	Rest	30 min run or walk	30 min run or walk	30 min walk	Rest or 30 min walk	**50-Mile / 100 km Race**	

100-Mile Training Plan

Month 1

	Mon	Tues	Wed	Thurs	Fri	Sat	Sun
Week 1	Rest	45 min run + 15 min weights	45 min run + 15 min weights Optional: speed work	45 min run + 15 min weights	1 hour run or cross-train	1 hour run	3 hour run
Week 2	Rest	45 min run + 15 min weights	45 min run + 15 min weights Optional: speed work	45 min run + 15 min weights	1 hour run or cross-train	1.5 hour run	3 hour run
Week 3 (Rest)	Rest	45 min run + 15 min weights	45 min run + 15 min weights Optional: speed work	45 min run + 15 min weights	1 hour run or cross-train	1 hour run	1.5 hour run
Week 4	Rest	45 min run + 15 min weights	45 min run + 15 min weights Optional: speed work	45 min run + 15 min weights	1 hour run or cross-train	2 hour run	3 hour run

Month 2

	Mon	Tues	Wed	Thurs	Fri	Sat	Sun
Week 5	Rest	45 min run + 15 min weights	45 min run + 15 min weights Optional: speed work	45 min run + 15 min weights	1 hour run or cross-train	3 hour run	3 hour run
Week 6 (Rest)	Rest	45 min run + 15 min weights	45 min run + 15 min weights Optional: speed work	45 min run + 15 min weights	1 hour run or cross-train	1 hour run	1.5 hour run
Week 7	Rest	45 min run + 15 min weights	45 min run + 15 min weights Optional: speed work	45 min run + 15 min weights	1 hour run or cross-train	3 hour run	4 hour run
Week 8	Rest	45 min run + 15 min weights	45 min run + 15 min weights Optional: speed work	45 min run + 15 min weights	1 hour run or cross-train	4 hour run	4 hour run

Month 3

	Mon	Tues	Wed	Thurs	Fri	Sat	Sun
Week 9 (Rest)	Rest	45 min run + 15 min weights	45 min run + 15 min weights Optional: speed work	45 min run + 15 min weights	1 hour run or cross-train	1 hour run	1.5 hour run
Week 10	Rest	45 min run + 15 min weights	45 min run + 15 min weights Optional: speed work	45 min run + 15 min weights	1 hour run or cross-train	4 hour run	4.5 hour run
Week 11	Rest	45 min run + 15 min weights	45 min run + 15 min weights Optional: speed work	45 min run + 15 min weights	1 hour run or cross-train	4 hour run	5 hour run
Week 12 (Taper)	Rest	1 hour run	1 hour run	1 hour run	1 hour run or cross-train	1 hour run	1.5 hour run
Week 13 (Taper)	Rest	1 hour run	1 hour run	30 min walk	Rest or 30 min walk	**100 Mile Race**	

Now that we have covered training plans in-depth, it is time to move on to ultramarathon racing. In the next chapter, we will discuss strategies and tactics to ensure you have the best possible experience on race day.

Ultramarathon Racing

After countless hours of training, it makes sense to invest the extra time needed for a smooth ultramarathon racing experience. This chapter covers the details on how to have the best race day possible, including race preparation, nutrition, and self-care.

Race Day Preparation

Arrive Early

Plan on arriving at least two hours before your race and even earlier if you are running 100 miles. Registering, pinning your race bib, and assembling your race gear all takes time. Rushing around is never fun and it adds extra stress on race day. Many runners choose to stay overnight at the race sight by camping or sleeping in their cars to avoid an early morning rush.

Pacers

Pacers are allowed for most 100-mile races and can usually join runners in the second half of the race. I always enjoy running with a pacer; however, some runners prefer to run solo. A pacer's job is to keep the runner company, to remind them to eat and drink, to set a reasonable pace, and to help navigate the course. Depending on race rules, pacers can also carry food, water, and gear for a runner. Due to time commitments, it's tough to find a pacer who can pace with you for more than a few hours. Many runners will organize a few pacers who can run different parts of the race with them.

Crew

Having at least one person support you is very helpful for races that take 24 hours or more to complete. Your crew's job is to assist with all your food, water, and gear. You never know what you are going to need during a 100-mile race, whether it's a battery charger for your phone or duct tape for your broken pole. Crews become very important in races with no aid stations, like the Badwater 135 in Death Valley. Runners get all their food and water from their crews in this race. Crews usually travel by car and meet their runner every hour or so.

Crewing sounds like easy work compared to running, yet crewing can be exhausting. In some races, crews need to drive hundreds of miles of back roads in the middle of the night to meet their runners.

Base Camp

Many ultramarathons are set up as loop systems—I ran my first 100-mile race on a 20-kilometre loop. My crew and I set up a large tent at the start/finish line that served as our base camp. I found it very helpful to have a convenient storage area for all my food, water, and gear. I also felt refreshed after spending time at base camp since it was familiar and I knew I could find my friends there.

Having a tent is helpful even if the race isn't set up as a loop system. It feels great to sleep in your tent after so many hours on your feet. Your tent might only be a small canvas layer, yet it can feel like a four-star hotel after or during an ultramarathon.

Race Nutrition

Nutrition and hydration can make or break your race and special planning is needed for these elements. Though improvisation is required during most races, below I've included some of the common issues that can arise and strategies on how to overcome these problems.

Butter tarts, burgers, potato chips, gummies, and doughnuts—these are all foods I have eaten during an ultramarathon. While I rarely eat these foods in everyday life, I like to let loose and eat as many calories as I can during a race. One of the reasons I love ultrarunning is that I can overindulge in food without gaining weight.

A runner can burn up to 16,000 calories during a 100-mile race, assuming that the race takes 27 hours to complete (Aschwanden 2008). Since an average meal has approximately 500 calories, an ultrarunner would need to eat 32 meals to replace the number of calories burned in a 100 miler. The truth is, you can't replace all the calories burned during a 100-mile race and you need to rely on your fat reserves for fuel. Food still plays an important role, however, and food becomes particularly important in the later stages of an ultramarathon. I usually feel very sluggish during the last few hours of a 100-mile or 100-kilometre race and I've found that eating something sugary will give me an immediate boost of energy.

Training to Eat and Run

A few years ago, I would get side cramps if I ran too soon after a meal; that was, until I read the book *Ultramarathon Man* by Dean Karnazes, one of the most well-known ultrarunners. In *Ultramarathon Man*, Karnazes explains that everyone can run after eating, you simply need to train for it. I took Karnazes's advice to heart and started running immediately after meals. After a few uncomfortable runs, my body got used to running on a full stomach and I no longer got side cramps. I am now able to easily eat large meals before or during a run. Just recently, I ate Thanksgiving dinner and went for a one-hour run not long afterwards.

Energy Gels

Energy gels are my favourite race food, since they are very convenient and they store well in my hydration pack. During a race, I'll eat roughly one energy gel every hour to ensure that my muscles have a steady supply of sugar. The first 10 energy gels taste okay, but after 20 hours I don't even want to look at a gel—the mouthful of super-sweet goo is almost too much to handle. You might be asking yourself how energy gels can be my favourite fuel source when I hate their taste. Gels are my favourite because I know they work. I have been racing with gels for over six years and gels have always helped get me through races.

Solid Food

In longer races, I like to eat solid food every few hours, especially at meal times. My body is used to eating breakfast, lunch, and dinner at the same time every day, and I start feeling sluggish if I don't eat during these times. One of my favourite solid food options is peanut butter and jam in a fajita wrap. I find fajitas easy to carry, as opposed to sandwiches that tend to get mashed to oblivion in my pack. Homemade chocolate chip cookies are another great option.

During a recent 100 miler, I brought six peanut butter and jam wraps and over 20 chocolate chip cookies. I loved the peanut butter and jam wraps but the chocolate chip cookies started to make me feel sick about halfway into the race. Improvising, I took advantage of the food at the aid stations. I ate small, cooked potatoes dipped in salt, warm grilled cheeses, and Timbits (doughnut holes). I was also drinking full cans of Coke or ginger ale every few hours. The carbonation and ginger in the ginger ale helped soothe my stomach. The huge amount of sugar and the caffeine in Coke gave me a great energy boost.

Stomach Problems

I'm fortunate to have what my family refers to as a cast-iron stomach. My gut can handle a lot of punishment and I rarely ever vomit. That being said, vomiting is a common occurrence during ultramarathons. I have seen runners toss their cookies in most of my longer races. A common piece of advice from professional ultrarunners is to never eat anything during a race that you haven't already tested during your training runs.

The standard protocol after vomiting is to get fluid and food back in your body as soon as you can. Since a runner has literally lost their lunch, hard work is needed to get the nutrition back in their body. I have seen runners test the waters after vomiting by sipping on ginger ale. If the soda stays down, they'll proceed to eat some solid food.

Diarrhea is also common in ultrarunning. Isn't this a great sport? Loose stools are normal during a race; however, runners should be wary of full-fledged diarrhea. Like the protocol after vomiting, you must make sure you are getting fluids back into your body if you have diarrhea while racing. Diarrhea can be avoided by sticking with familiar foods pre-race and during the race. Eating in unknown restaurants and eating new foods before and during a race are surefire ways to get the runs (pun intended).

Dehydration

Dehydration is normal during an ultramarathon; however, hydration should be managed very carefully since severe dehydration can lead to serious health problems. I monitor the colour of my urine during a race to gauge my level of hydration. I know that I'm sufficiently hydrated if I'm peeing every one and a half hours or so and if my urine is the colour of lemonade (the yellow kind). If my pee is a shade of orange, I know that I'm pushing my limits. When this happens, I'll usually take two salt pills and will increase the amount of water I'm drinking. I'll aim to drink all the water I have with me before I reach the next aid station and I'll proceed to drink at least a full litre of water when I reach the aid station. It's important to have salt/electrolytes with water. Your body can't replace water effectively without salt. I take one to two salt pills every 45 minutes during a race.

Bloody urine is a sign of severe hydration and kidney distress. When this happens, runners should drop out of their race and seek medical attention. I had a scary experience at the Sulphur Springs 50 km in 2016, which I described earlier in the book. Getting severely dehydrated, I ended the race peeing blood and feeling awful. I was really shaken up after the race but I've learned some very important lessons as a result. I now take extra precautions to stay hydrated, including carrying extra water during hot weather and taking salt pills on a regular basis.

Self-Care

Nipple Chafing

Chafing is not a big deal for training runs but it can easily ruin your day during a race. As funny as nipple chafing might sound, it is a painful and upsetting condition that needs to be managed properly. I protect my nipples with small adhesive plastic discs, designed specifically for endurance athletes.

Lubrication

Monkey butt and chub rub—these glamorous sounding conditions can be very painful. Monkey butt occurs when you get chafing between your buttocks. The dreaded chub rub occurs from chafing on your undercarriage. Fortunately, preventative lubrication down south can spare you from these afflictions. I prefer to use a natural lubricant with a coconut oil base since I don't feel good about putting a petroleum-based product on my nether regions.

Foot Care

Ultrarunners love to share photos of their gnarly feet on social media. Rarely does a week go by that I don't see a picture of an ultrarunner's messed-up feet on my Instagram feed. Losing toenails and getting blisters are inevitable in ultrarunning, but there are ways to lessen the pain.

As described in the running gear section, a shoe with a large toe box is the key for decreasing your chances of losing toenails. Large toe boxes keep your toenails from pounding into the front of your shoe. Ultrarunning legend Marshall Ulrich got so sick of losing his toenails that he had them surgically removed in 1992. Ulrich describes his surgery and his reasons for the procedure in his great book about running across America, *Running on Empty*.

Blisters can be just as painful as losing toenails but there are ways to prevent blisters from forming. Applying lubrication or tape to hotspots can help prevent or lessen blisters. Hotspots are sore areas on your feet which have not yet become full-fledged blisters. Hotspots often develop on your heel, the bottom of your midfoot, and the outside of your big toes and pinky toes.

Keeping your feet dry during a race also helps. Getting wet feet is unavoidable for most trail races; however, I limit the damage by changing socks on a regular basis. There are runners who also change shoes but this practice is controversial. Some ultrarunners say that you should never change shoes in a race and other runners have no problem with it.

I have run with good-sized blisters for all my longer races and have learned that sometimes I just need to tune out the pain. That being said, you should speak with the medical staff if your feet start feeling really bad. Most race volunteers are experienced in foot care.

Heatstroke

Mild heatstroke is common in ultrarunning and can be treated fairly easily. Some of the mild heatstroke symptoms that I've experienced include dizziness, nausea, headache, and fatigue. I can usually bounce back from these symptoms if I drink extra water and slow my pace. I'll also take advantage of rivers and lakes along a race course by splashing water on my face and the back of my neck.

If symptoms don't improve after an hour or so, a runner might have severe heatstroke. Feeling confused or agitated can often accompany a bad case of heatstroke (Mayo Clinic n.d.). Severe heatstroke is a serious condition and should be treated accordingly. If you reach this point, I would suggest dropping out of the race and getting medical attention.

The good news is that runners can train to handle the heat. To prepare for races in hot weather, I'll do my longer training sessions in the full heat of the day. I start with shorter training sessions in the heat and build my way up to longer ones. Using this method, I've since successfully completed several races in the heat.

Injuries

Expect minor injuries during trail races. I've fallen down several times, which resulted in small cuts, bruises, and sprains. I don't think it's worth it, however, to test your limits with major injuries like broken bones. My personal rule is that I'll drop out of a race if I suffer an injury that will stop me from training for more than a month. I love to race, but I love to train even more. I rely heavily on my regular runs to clear my head, lift my mood, and relieve stress. I'm very reluctant to do anything that will take running away for a long time.

Up to this point, we have covered all the material needed for a runner to have a great first ultramarathon experience. In the next chapter, we cover material that will help you with your longevity in ultrarunning. Since ultrarunning is such a demanding sport, you will need to ensure that you are giving your body the fuel it needs for training and recovery. The Nutrition and Health section outlines my current eating and wellness practices, which have helped me continuously improve at ultrarunning over the last six years.

Nutrition and Health

At 40 years old, I have more energy than ever and I attribute this in large part to my daily eating habits. I eat highly nutritious foods at every meal, which fuels my active lifestyle and helps my body recover from training. This chapter outlines the three big lessons I've learned about healthy eating, along with my current tactics for maintaining a healthy weight and fueling a very active lifestyle. My goal for this chapter is to share the nutrition practices that have given me longevity in ultrarunning, so that you, too, can continue running ultramarathons over the years.

Three Big Lessons for Healthy Eating

Big Lesson #1: Mindful Eating

Low fat, low carb and keto diets—I have had tried all of them. Although these diets have helped me reach a healthier weight at different times of my life, I believe that they are unnecessary and potentially dangerous ways of eating. I have recently learned that restrictive diets like low carb can negatively affect your relationship with food and potentially lead to eating disorders. I know

now that you can enjoy all types of food with mindful eating. I practice mindful eating by cutting unnecessary snacks and through slow and deliberate eating at mealtimes.

On a day where I'm not training for more than two-hours, I get all the nutrition that I need from three meals, and I won't have any snacks. Leading up to the Midnight Moose 100 Miler in September 2019, I lost over 15 pounds of excess body fat by cutting out unnecessary snacks. Prior to that, I ate high-calorie snacks first thing in the morning and before bed, along with random snacks throughout the day. I was ingesting a ton of calories without realizing it because I was eating so frequently. I certainly support the practice of eating when you are hungry, especially during heavy training days. In my case though, I was eating high calorie snacks out of habit and not because I was hungry.

I also practice slow and deliberate eating during mealtime so I can enjoy my food and monitor my level of satiety. My favourite meal tastes even better when I take the time to enjoy each bite. After I've eaten a reasonably sized portion, I'll load up my plate again if I'm still hungry. I know that I can trust my feelings of hunger if I'm eating slowly.

Big Lesson #2: Stay on Track with Goals

The best way to add focus and discipline to my nutrition is to sign up for a race. Paying the race's registration fee and getting the race's confirmation email solidifies my commitment to my goal of completing the race. Once I have a race in my calendar, I'm dedicated to doing what's necessary to lessen the impending pain that comes with an ultramarathon and to perform to the best of my abilities.

Although all ultramarathons are painful, carrying excess weight makes an ultramarathon even more painful. The avoidance of this extra pain acts as a potent motivator. When I'm tempted to eat a bowl of ice cream after dinner, even though I'm perfectly full, I'll think of the added suffering that I might be causing in my future race.

I'm also extremely motivated by wanting to perform well in a race. Eating highly nutritious foods speeds up my recovery from training and protects me from getting sick. When I eat well, I'm giving my body all that it needs to recuperate from heavy training and to prepare for a strong finish in my upcoming ultramarathon.

Big Lesson #3: Healthy Eating is the Key to a Healthy Weight

I was fortunate to learn early in life that I needed more than regular exercise to maintain a healthy weight. When I was overweight in high school, I attempted to get in shape through only exercise, without making any changes to my poor food choices. Thankfully, my dad pointed me in the right direction when I expressed my frustration that I wasn't losing any weight despite all my efforts at the gym. The pounds melted away once I started paying attention to my portion sizes at meals. The combination of solid nutrition and working out produced big results and I lost over 70 pounds in one year.

Tactics for Healthy Eating

The Big-Ass Salad

The term "big-ass salad" was coined by Mark Sisson, a fitness author and former ironman triathlete. I've been eating a big-ass salad for lunch every day for the last few years. Prior to big-ass salads, my lunch of choice was a ham and cheese sandwich. Although ham and cheese is delicious, these sandwiches left me wanting a snack by mid-afternoon. Big-ass salads, however, keep me full until supper time.

I load my big-ass salad with kale and spinach. With a great amount of fibre, antioxidants, calcium, vitamins, and minerals, these leafy greens are some of the most nutritious foods on the planet. It's also important to eat organic since conventional kale and spinach are higher in pesticides. Kale and spinach have a lot of fibre, and fibre binds water and expands in your gut, making you feel full. High-fibre foods are also very good for gut health. Fibre feeds good gut bacteria and helps you have regular bowel movements (Everyday Health 2019).

All the chewing used to eat a big salad is also beneficial. There is good scientific evidence that the more you chew, the fuller you feel (Miquel-Kergoat et al. 2015). Although the ham and cheese sandwich has the same number of calories as the big-ass salad, the sandwich only takes a few bites to eat.

Supplements

I worked in the supplements industry for several years and have learned a lot about different supplements and their benefits. I'm a big believer in getting most of my nutrition from food; however, I have a few go-to supplements.

Fish Oil

Fish oil is loaded with omega-3 fatty acids, which have several benefits for brain and body health. There is good preliminary evidence that fish oil helps with brain injury recovery (Gupta, Summerville, and Senter 2019).

I have been taking fish oil regularly for the last two years and I believe that fish oil has helped me build back my brain health. In the Introduction chapter, I described the significant concussion that I suffered in my first year of university. In the years after that concussion, I would get post-concussion syndrome (PCS) symptoms from insignificant blows to the head. If I hit my head while getting something out of the car, I would have the foggy feeling for a few days. Since taking fish oil, I can now withstand a good-sized bump to the head without any PCS symptoms.

Fish oil has also been linked to speeding muscle recovery after a workout. Omega-3 fatty acids are used to repair muscle cell walls. These fatty acids also help to relieve inflammation, which can speed the healing process and relieve joint pain after a workout (Sherrell 2021).

Vitamin D

Vitamin D is known to benefit mental health, bone health, and cardiovascular health. Though the need to supplement with vitamin D has come under scrutiny over the last few years, I continue to take vitamin D during the winter months. Vitamin D is produced when your skin gets exposed to the sun. The shorter days and less skin exposed to the sun in the winter means that my body is producing less vitamin D than in the warmer months.

Probiotics

Probiotics are beneficial bacteria that are naturally present in our digestive tracts. Probiotics have been linked to several different health benefits that include improving digestive health, boosting immunity (Brown 2016), and potentially even improving mental health (Clapp et al. 2017). I like to get probiotics from fermented foods like organic and unpasteurized sauerkraut. I'll often include a few tablespoons of sauerkraut with my salads. My daily helping of sauerkraut has a similar amount of probiotic as a typical probiotic supplement, while also including a healthy dose of vitamins, minerals, and fibre.

I have been told that making sauerkraut is quite easy but I've never done it. In the production of sauerkraut, shredded cabbage is sealed in a glass jar in saltwater brine. In around a week's time, naturally occurring probiotic bacteria, like *Lactobacillus*, multiply and ferment the cabbage, transforming it into sauerkraut. The gut-friendly bacteria remain present after the main fermentation and during all the sauerkraut's shelf life. Significant amounts of probiotic are only found in unpasteurized sauerkraut. Due to its live bacterial culture, unpasteurized sauerkraut needs to be refrigerated. Pasteurized and shelf-stable sauerkraut does not have a significant amount of probiotic.

Plant-Based Eating

Some of the top ultrarunners in the world follow plant-based diets. Scott Jurek, who many consider the best ultrarunner of all time, follows a strict vegan diet. A vegan diet means eliminating any animal-based products from your diet, including meat, dairy, eggs, and honey. Eating a plant-based diet means getting the majority of your nutrition from plants while still having the option to eat a small amount of animal-based products.

While I still eat animal-based food, over the years I've increased the amount of plant-based food that I eat. I believe that eating a large amount of plant-based food helps me recover quickly from demanding ultramarathon training. I eat vegetarian meals for breakfast and lunch and I am working on finding more plant-based dinners that my whole family can enjoy.

Plant-based diets also have huge benefits for the environment. Studies have shown that plant-based diets could "add up to 49 percent to the global food supply without expanding croplands" (Jalava, Kummu and Porkka 2014).

Eating a plant-based diet also significantly reduces carbon emissions and freshwater usage (Hunnes n.d.). What's more, plant-based eating helps to significantly reduce harm to animals. Simply put, eating a plant-based diet means that fewer animals are killed for food.

Managing Stress

Stress is one of my biggest triggers for weight gain and I tend to pack on the pounds during stressful times at work, even when I'm eating well. High stress levels can increase the level of the hormone cortisol in your blood, which has been linked to slowing down your metabolism (Preiato 2020). I find that I eat more food than usual when I'm stressed. My stomach and brain tell me that I'm hungry even though I know that I have eaten enough.

Managing stress is one of the key elements of my ultraliving lifestyle. I have worked hard to avoid being overly stressed in the last few years. My keys to fighting stress overload are daily exercise, daily stretching, meditation, massage, journaling, and mindful breathing.

Daily Exercise, Stretching, and Massage

Running is my natural choice for daily exercise. My one-hour run at lunch clears my mind and splits up my day. On very busy days, I run in silence, without music, to give my mind an extra break.

As I have gotten older, stretching and foam rolling have become critical components of my training. Due to the nature of my job, I spend a large part of my day seated at a desk. The long periods of sitting, coupled with all my running, can easily lead to a decreased range of motion and injury. To avoid injury, I do a 15-minute routine of stretching and foam rolling every evening, focusing on my legs and lower back. I always feel more relaxed after my routine; stretching helps me calm my mind and prevents worry about injury.

Finally, massage is an amazing tool for relaxation and injury prevention. I have recently started getting a monthly one-hour massage and it has been a game changer for stress relief and for keeping my running strains to a minimum.

Meditation and Mindful Running

I handle stress much better when I incorporate a 15-minute meditation session into my day. I pick a quiet spot where I won't be interrupted, usually my bedroom, and I sit with my legs crossed and my back leaned against the wall. The purists say that you should sit in Half Lotus without any back support but I find this too uncomfortable. Once situated, I focus on my breathing, taking normal-sized breaths in and out through my nose. I alternate between keeping my eyes open and closed. When keeping my eyes open, I'll focus on a tree branch, some plants, or a patch of blue sky. When I inevitably get distracted by a random thought, I simply observe the thought and then let it go. I remind myself that I'm practicing and that it takes time to train my mind. While I'm meditating, I like to repeat a mantra in my mind to enhance the experience. I'll repeat "so hum," which is an ancient mantra that means "I am that," often interpreted to mean that I am one with the universe.

Meditation doesn't have to take the form of sitting still. I also practice mindful running, which is a great way to find time for meditation on busy days. Similar to sitting meditation, I focus my attention on my breathing while I run. I let my breathing happen naturally, not limiting it in any way. Once I've focused on my breathing for five minutes, I'll draw my attention to the movement of my body. I feel my feet striking the ground, my arms swinging, and my core muscles tightening. I reflect on how amazing it is that my body knows how to run without consciously thinking about it. I usually practice mindful running for 15 minutes during my regular one-hour run.

Journaling

I write in my journal every day for 15 minutes. It took some practice to get into the routine but it is now effortless. I keep the pressure low for journaling and just write whatever is on my mind. I usually write about the highlights and the issues of my previous day. I'll include a note about the progress that I've made on my goals as well. For example, I'll note that I completed my training goals for the week and that I'm happy about it. I've recently started journaling about the person who I'd like to become, not just the completion of my goals but also the virtues I'd like to develop. One of the virtues that I'm currently working on is to always keep my cool around my family. I want to set a positive example for them by staying calm under pressure.

I also practice gratitude daily by writing a few sentences. I like to pick something basic, something special, and something related to family. For example, I'll write that I'm grateful for the clean air that we breathe, I'm grateful that I'm going to a concert with friends this week and that I take the time to appreciate art and life, and I'm grateful for the health of my wife and my kids.

Mindful Breathing

On very busy days, I often catch myself holding my breath. Understandably, holding my breath adds to anxious feelings, since my body depends on breathing for all its vital processes. I check in a few times during the day to ensure that I'm breathing properly, ensuring that I'm engaging my diaphragm and taking deep enough breaths through my nose. These check-ins only take 10 seconds but they do a lot for reducing stress.

Managing stress is an element that is not typically covered in an ultramarathon training plan; however, it is an important component to ultraliving. I've spent extra time on this topic with the hope that my tools for managing stress will help runners who are struggling to maintain a healthy weight. Managing stress also has the amazing benefit of bringing more joy into your life. Great things happen when you control and quiet your mind.

Although nutrition and health alone will not allow you to complete an ultramarathon, they are critical components to setting up a solid foundation for ultrarunning. An athlete can run a single ultramarathon with poor nutrition; however, it will be very difficult to sustain the practice over the years without proper nutrition and weight management.

While this chapter has described how to nourish your body, the next chapter will help nourish your soul. In the upcoming Inspiration chapter, I list the personalities in ultrarunning who have motivated me the most over the last six years. While this chapter is not critical for ultramarathon preparation, I believe that the stories shared will help drive your training and give you the energy needed to lace up your shoes for your training runs every day.

Inspiration

Ultrarunning Influencers

This chapter is made up of brief descriptions of the running careers of some of my favourite ultrarunners, along with a curated list of their books, quotes, podcasts, and movies. This short list of athletes includes Ray Zahab, Scott Jurek, Kilian Jornet, Dean Karnazes, Courtney Dauwalter, Karl Meltzer, Ann Trason, David Goggins, and Gary Robbins. I derive a large amount of motivation by following these amazing athletes and I'm glad to share short summaries of their impressive accomplishments.

Ray Zahab

I've included Ray as the first athlete on this list because I have a personal relationship with him. I've been very fortunate to have kept in touch with Ray since I ran one of his races in Gatineau, Quebec in 2019. Ray has been extremely supportive of my running and has given me invaluable advice and encouragement over the last few years.

As mentioned earlier in this book, Ray is among the most accomplished Canadian adventurers of all time. Ray is most well-known for running and completing the 7,500 kilometre Sahara Desert in 111 days in 2006. This amazing trek was the basis for the movie *Running the Sahara*, which was narrated and produced by Academy Award–winner Matt Damon.

Now, at over 50 years old, Ray doesn't show any signs of slowing down. In January 2020, Ray crossed Baffin Island in the extreme cold while dragging all his supplies in a sled. In August 2021, Ray attempted a self-supported crossing of Death Valley on foot; however, he needed to stop in the end due to the extreme heat and lack of water.

Books

> *Running for My Life* (2007)
> *Running to Extremes* (co-author) (2011)
> *Just Deserts* (co-author) (2011)

Favourite Quote

"Ultrarunning is 90 percent mental, the other 10 percent is all in our heads!" (Zahab n.d.)

Social Media

> Instagram: @rayzahab
> Facebook: Ray Zahab

Podcasts

> *Explore: A Canadian Geographic podcast* on April 11, 2019
> *Human Performance Outliers Podcast* on June 4, 2021

Movies

> *Running the Sahara* (2007)

Scott Jurek

Scott Jurek is one of the top trail runners of all time. In Jurek's prime, he won most of the top trail races in the world, including the technical Hardrock 100 and the speedy Western States 100. Hardrock 100 and Western States are generally considered the North American trail running championships. Jurek won the Western States 100 a record seven times in a row from 1999 to 2005. He is a passionate plant-based athlete and credits much of his success to his vegan diet.

Jurek gained a huge amount of popularity after being featured in Christopher McDougall's book *Born to Run*. Shortly after *Born to Run's* release, Jurek went on to write his own book, *Eat and Run*, which is a memoir about Jurek's childhood and development as an ultrarunner. Jurek co-authored his second book, *North*, with his wife Jenny. *North* tells the story of Scott and Jenny working together so Scott could set the fastest known time for the 3,523-kilometre Appalachian Trail in 2015.

Books

Eat and Run (2012)
North (2018)

Favourite Quote

"The longer and farther I ran, the more I realized that what I was often chasing was a state of mind—a place where worries that seemed monumental melted away." (Jurek and Friedman 2012, 181)

This quote is a great description for one of the main reasons that I run. It's amazing how worries go away, tough issues sort themselves out, and a poor mindset can be replaced by a good one. I like to tell people that running is my therapy. Although I say this as a joke, there is a lot of truth to it. Modern life is very stressful, whether it's stress from work or family. Without close attention, stress can cause you to pack on the pounds and get out of shape. Running lets me deal with this stress while simultaneously helping me stay in shape.

Social Media

Instagram: @scottjurek

Podcasts

    Billy Yang Podcast on May 3, 2018
    Ginger Runner LIVE on April 8, 2019

Movies

    The Game Changers (2018)

Jurek is featured among other plant-based athletes who are at the top of their sports. This movie does a great job showing that athletes can be world-class while eating a vegan diet.

Kilian Jornet

Known simply as Kilian in the ultrarunning community, Kilian Jornet is a trail running icon. He has won a very large number of ultramarathons, including Hardrock 100, Western States 100, and Ultra-Trail du Mont-Blanc (UTMB). Even after racing at a high level for over 20 years, Kilian is still considered as a favourite for any race that he enters. Kilian is literally at home in the mountains. He was raised by his parents in a refuge at 2,000 metres in the Spanish Pyrenees Mountains.

Books

    Run or Die (2011)
    La Frontera Invisible (Spanish and French only) (2013)
    Summits of My Life (2018)
    Training for the Uphill Athlete (co-author) (2019)

Favourite Quote

"The secret isn't in your legs, but in your strength of mind. You need to go for a run when it is raining, windy, and snowing, when lightning sets trees on fire as you pass them" (Jornet 2013)

Social Media

>Instagram: @kilianjornet
>Facebook: Kilian Jornet

Movies

>*Unbreakable: The Western States 100* (2011)

Unbreakable tells the story of the four front-runners of the 2010 Western States 100: Hal Koerner, Anton Krupicka, Geoff Roes, and Kilian Jornet. At the time of the movie, Koerner was the two-time defending champion, and Krupicka, Roes and Kilian had been winning most of the trail races they'd entered. Watching these four incredibly talented runners battle it out is very exciting. Complete with unexpected twists and turns, this movie is definitely a trail-running classic.

Dean Karnazes

Dean Karnazes is one of the most well-known ultrarunning figures in the world. Written in 2006, Karnazes's book *Ultramarathon Man* outlines a very impressive list of accomplishments. Many ultrarunners credit *Ultramarathon Man* for inspiring them to run their first ultramarathon. In addition to winning the Badwater 135 in 2003 and 2004, Karnazes has run 50 marathons in 50 different states in 50 days and set a world record for running 350 miles straight.

Books

>*Ultramarathon Man* (2006)
>*50/50* (2009)
>*Run!* (2011)
>*The Road to Sparta* (2016)

Favourite Quote

"Run when you can, walk if you have to, crawl if you must; just never give up." (Karnazes 2006, 278)

Karnazes includes this as advice for first-time ultramarathon runners since dropping out of races is a common occurrence in ultrarunning. Many runners feel like giving up mid-race because of the extreme amount of stress—the fatigue, nausea, and pain. But a beautiful thing about ultrarunning is that an extreme low point is almost always temporary. If I feel like giving up, I'll have something to eat, find someone to talk to, and, like magic, the negative feelings will dissipate. The more races that I complete, the less I feel like quitting when races become difficult.

Social Media

>Instagram: @ultramarathon
>Facebook: Dean Karnazes

Podcasts

>*Rich Roll Podcast* on November 28, 2016
>*Trail Runner Nation* on September 1, 2017
>*Ginger Runner LIVE* on July 2, 2018

Movies

>*Ultramarathon Man:50 Marathons, 50 States, 50 Days* (2008)

Courtney Dauwalter

Courtney Dauwalter is currently considered one of the world's top ultrarunners. In 2018, Dauwalter won the well-known Moab 240 trail race and placed first for women in the 2018 Western States 100, with the second fastest time ever. In 2019, Dauwalter finished in first place for women at the 2019 Ultra-Trail du Mont-Blanc and first overall for the United States Big's Backyard Ultra. The rules of Big's Backyard are simple: runners must complete a 6.7-kilometre loop every hour until there is one person left standing. Dauwalter ran an incredible 456 kilometres in 68 hours.

In addition to her impressive running accomplishments, Dauwalter is known for her positive attitude, grit, and for running in stereotype-busting basketball shorts. One of her sponsors, Salomon, made custom running shorts for Dauwalter in the basketball style. Dauwalter is also known for fueling with mashed potatoes during her races. She and her crew preload mashed potatoes into squeeze packs before races.

Favourite Quote

"I love the feeling of running and of enjoying the outdoors. I do my best thinking while I'm out moving silently across the trails." (Superfeet 2018)

Like Dauwalter, I love the feeling of being alone and moving fast on the trails. I feel joy and excitement when I'm trail running, similar to the feelings I remember when playing a great game as a child. I also do a lot of thinking while I'm out running. Without meaning to, my brain will start solving tough issues and I come back from a run feeling lighter and relieved.

Social Media

    Instagram: @courtneydauwalter
    Facebook: Courtney Dauwalter

Podcasts

    Billy Yang Podcast on September 26, 2018 and March 18, 2019
    Ginger Runner LIVE on November 13, 2017, June 25, 2018, and September 9, 2019
    The Joe Rogan Experience on October 24, 2017

Movies

    The Source (2019) (found on YouTube)

A short documentary on Courtney's attempt to win the 2018 Tahoe 200, the movie *The Source* also explores the source of Courtney's inspiration, grit, and determination that enables her to run and win these amazingly tough races.

Karl Meltzer

Karl Meltzer, also known as the "Speedgoat," is one of my favourite runners. Meltzer has a no-nonsense attitude and keeps ultrarunning very simple. He doesn't have a complicated training or nutrition plan; he just puts in the work.

Meltzer has the most 100-mile victories ever. He has won Hardrock 100 five times and set the FKT for the 3,523-kilometre Appalachian Trail in 2016. Meltzer's FKT has since been broken a number of times.

Favourite Quote

"One hundred miles isn't that far." (Mock 2014)

This is Meltzer's signature quote—he mentions it during most podcast interviews. While 100 miles seems like an extremely long distance, it actually isn't that far in the grand scheme of your life. The average Canadian's lifetime is made up of 732,000 hours (Macrotrends 2022) and it will likely take you around 27 hours to finish a 100-mile race.

Podcasts

Ginger Runner LIVE on June 18, 2018

Movies

Karl Meltzer: Made to Be Broken (2016)

The movie is the story of Meltzer's Appalachian Trail FKT and can be found on the Red Bull website or Vimeo.

Ann Trason

At 61 years old, Ann Trason is one of the most accomplished ultrarunners of our time. Trason might be best known for her performances at the Western States 100, a race in which she was the top female 14 times. Although Trason never won Western States outright, she came in second place overall two times and placed in the top six overall eight times. Trason is so enamored with Western States that she moved to Auburn, California, where the race takes place annually.

With its release in 2009, Christopher McDougall's famous book *Born to Run* brought international notoriety to Ann Trason. In the book, McDougall describes Trason's showdown with Tarahumara runners at the 1994 Leadville 100, one of the world's toughest 100-mile races. The Tarahumara are an Indigenous tribe of "running people" from the Copper Canyon region of Mexico.

Favourite Quote

"I've always just looked at 100 miles as life in a day. You have all the trials and tribulations of a life in one day." (Strout 2015)

Many ultrarunners describe the significant highs and lows that they experience during a 100-mile race. I've experienced these highs and lows a number of times during longer races. I'll feel amazing at 50 kilometres, terrible at 100 kilometres, only to feel amazing again while finishing the race at 160 kilometres. In our lives, we've all gone through dark periods and periods of joy, albeit on a much larger time frame. A 100-mile race allows you to experience the emotional extremes of life in one day.

Podcasts

Ginger Runner LIVE on March 5, 2018

Movies

15 Hours with Ann Trason (2015) (by Billy Yang and found on YouTube)

David Goggins

David Goggins is an ultraendurance athlete, author, motivational speaker, and a former Navy SEAL. I have listened to Goggins's audiobook *Can't Hurt Me* at least three times since I discovered it in 2019. Goggins finished third overall in the Badwater 135 in 2007. In 2013, Goggins broke the world record for the most pull-ups in 24 hours, completing 4,030.

Books

Can't Hurt Me (2018)

Favourite Quote

"Only when you identify and accept your weaknesses will you finally stop running from your past. Then those incidents can be used more efficiently as fuel to become better and grow stronger." (Goggins 2018, 147)

This quote has special meaning to me since it reflects my experience in writing this book. I felt exhausted after writing about my struggles with my weight. I now feel like I have finally left these problems in the past and that I have freed up the emotional energy I need to accomplish my big plans for the future.

Social Media

>Instagram: @davidgoggins
>Facebook: David Goggins

Podcasts

>*Rich Roll Podcast* on January 2, 2017
>*Rich Roll Podcast* on January 1, 2019

Gary Robbins

Gary Robbins is one of the most well-known Canadian ultrarunners. He's the star of the movie *Where Dreams Go to Die*, which documents Gary's attempts at the infamous Barkley Marathons.

Robbins grew up in Mount Pearl, Newfoundland and left to Whistler, British Columbia in his early twenties to pursue adventure racing. After a few adventure races, Robbins found out that he had a real talent for trail running and decided to enter some races. Robbins entered his first 100 miler in Squamish, BC in 2008 and surprised himself by winning it and setting a course record.

Building up steam after Squamish, Robbins won and set the course record for Hawaii's HURT Trail 100-Mile Endurance Run (HURT 100) in 2010. Robbins won HURT 100 again in 2013. Continuing to have success in running, Robbins entered the Barkley Marathons in 2016. After failing to complete the Barkley Marathons, Robbins entered it again in 2017. These two attempts at the race are the basis for the 2018 movie *Where Dreams Go to Die*.

The movie helped elevate Robbins to one of the most well-known ultrarunners in the sport. It also led to the documentary *Endless*, which aired across Canada on The Sports Network (TSN).

Robbins is one of the race directors for Coast Mountain Trail Running, an organization that puts on a series of races in British Columbia. Squamish 50 is their most popular race, taking place on the very tough but beautiful trails of Squamish.

Favourite Quote

"An unwavering dedication to a goal, high pain tolerance, mental strength and resilience, ability to rally from deep lows in an expeditious manner, and a really good appetite." (Canadian Running 2018)

This is Robbins's response to being asked what his defining characteristics are as a runner in a March 2018 interview with Canadian Running Magazine. I love that Robbins mentions a really good appetite. A love of food is common among ultrarunners—you often see photos of doughnuts, pancakes, and beer on the Instagram pages of runners. One of the reasons that I love ultrarunning is that I can eat a lot of delicious food guilt free.

Social Media

 Instagram: @garyrobbins
 Facebook: Gary Robbins

Podcasts

 Ginger Runner LIVE on May 16, 2017
 Ginger Runner LIVE on December 16, 2019

Movies

 Where Dreams Go to Die (2018)

Final Thoughts

Although ultrarunning is an extreme sport, it does not mean that you should be unkind to yourself. I certainly push my limits as a runner; however, I do my best to explore my limits in a safe and healthy manner. Most ultrarunners are like me and have life commitments and people who depend on them. We can't afford to be taken out of our lives due to a significant injury. It makes for a good story to hear about how a runner passed out on the side of the road during a race due to exhaustion and dehydration, but I would rather be known as the runner who was prepared and completed the race.

One of the main reasons I called this book "ultraliving" is because the title has "living" in it. It's important to distinguish between learning about ultramarathons and the actual living of an ultramarathon, which includes training and racing. I'm an avid reader and I love to learn everything I can about a subject when embarking on a new interest or project. Over the years, there have been times that I've fallen into the trap of continuing to read and to learn about a subject even after I've gathered all the lessons that I need. I encourage you to put into practice what you've learned in this book by signing up for a race. If you are new to running, you can take the first step by signing up for a 5-kilometre or 10-kilometre race. If you have been running for some time and feel that you are ready, consider signing up for your first 50-kilometre race. Having a race in your calendar helps you truly tap into all the Ultraliving Lessons that you've learned about. Start your ultraliving journey by planning your training months in advance, following through on your plan, and completing your race in a fashion that you can be proud of. If you don't succeed at completing your race, that's okay, you can try again. After all, one of the main themes in ultraliving is perseverance. Even if you have a terrible experience during your first ultramarathon, there is something about ultrarunning that can make you look back on the experience with fondness. It just takes time to put things into perspective.

It is also important to remember that ultraliving is a practice, just like lawyers practice law and doctors practice medicine. I continue to learn and to evolve in my ultraliving experience. I continue to find new ways to motivate, to prepare, and to persevere.

Returning to the term "living," ultraliving is focused on running but its practice will improve your overall life. Patience, gratitude, and the ability to stay calm under pressure are only a few of the virtues that I've developed through ultrarunning. Most importantly, ultraliving doesn't have to be complicated, and you can start your journey by simply lacing up your shoes and going for a short run. If you can't run for more than a few minutes, that's fine, alternate between running and walking. No matter what kind of shape you're in or what your life circumstances are, the most important part of ultraliving is to start.

It was one of the best decisions of my life.

References

Aschwanden, Christie. (2008). "How To Fuel Up During An Ultra." Runner's World, March 10, 2008. Accessed January 12, 2022. https://www.runnersworld.com/training/a20808916/how-to-fuel-up-during-an-ultra-marathon/.

Bartholomew, Lucy. (2019). "Week 1 word: ready?" Lucy Bartholomew, June 25, 2019. Accessed January 12, 2022. https://www.lucybartholomew.com/week-1-word-ready

Brick, Noel E., Megan J. McElhinney, and Richard S. Metcalfe. (2018). "The effects of facial expression and relaxation cues on movement economy, physiological, and perceptual responses during running." Psychology of Sport and Exercise 34: 20–28. https://doi.org/10.1016/j.psychsport.2017.09.009

Brown, Mary Jane. (2016). "8 Health Benefits of Probiotics." Healthline, August 23, 2016. Accessed January 14, 2022. https://www.healthline.com/nutrition/8-health-benefits-of-probiotics#TOC_TITLE_HDR_1.

Canadian Running. (2018). "10 questions with Gary Robbins." Canadian Running, March 8, 2018. Accessed January 17, 2022. https://runningmagazine.ca/trail-running/10-questions-gary-robbins/.

Clapp, Megan, Nadia Aurora, Lindsey Herrera, Manisha Bhatia, Emily Wilen, and Sarah Wakefield. (2017). "Gut microbiota's effect on mental health: The gut-brain axis." Clinics and Practice 7(987):131–136. https://dx.doi.org/10.4081%2Fcp.2017.987

Coelho, Paulo. (2014). The Alchemist. New York: HarperCollins.

Cohen, Joel H. (2017). How to Lose a Marathon: A Starter's Guide to Finishing 26.2 Chapters. New York: Abrams Image.

Cooper, Bob. (2021). "Exactly How to Taper for a Marathon." Runner's World, September 24, 2021. Accessed January 12, 2022. https://www.runnersworld.com/training/a20802690/why-you-should-taper-before-a-marathon/.

Everyday Health. (2019). "Why Is Fiber Important for Your Digestive Health?" Everyday Health. June 6, 2019. Accessed January 13, 2022. https://www.everydayhealth.com/digestive-health/experts-why-is-fiber-important.aspx

Goggins, David. (2018). Can't Hurt Me:Master Your Mind and Defy the Odds. Carson City, Nevada: Lioncrest Publishing.

Gupta, Anjali, Greg Summerville, and Carlin Senter. (2019). "Treatment of Acute Sports–Related Concussion." Current Reviews in Musculoskeletal Medicine 12(2):117–123. https://doi.org/10.1007/s12178-019-09545-7

Hadfield, Chris. (2015). An Astronaut's Guide to Life on Earth. Toronto: Random House of Canada.

Harvard Health Publishing. (2016). "Preserve your muscle mass." Harvard Health Publishing. February 19, 2016. Accessed January 12, 2022. https://www.health.harvard.edu/staying-healthy/preserve-your-muscle-mass

Hill, Napoleon. (1928). The Law of Success: in Sixteen Lessons. Meriden: The Ralston University Press.

House, Steve, Scott Johnston, and Kilian Jornet. (2019). Training for the Uphill Athlete: A Manual for Mountain Runners & Ski Mountaineers. Ventura, CA: Patagonia Books.

Hunnes, Dana. n.d. "The Case for Plant Based." UCLA Sustainability. Accessed January 14, 2022. https://www.sustain.ucla.edu/food-systems/the-case-for-plant-based/.

Jalava, M., Kummu, M., Porkka, M., Siebert, S. and Varis, O. (2014). "Diet change—a solution to reduce water use?" Environmental Research Letters 9(5). https://iopscience.iop.org/article/10.1088/1748-9326/9/7/074016

Johansson, Jorgen. (2010). Smarter Backpacking: Or How Every Backpacker Can Apply Lightweight Trekking and Ultralight Hiking Techniques. Akersberga, Sweden: Nui AB.

Johansson, Jörgen. (2019). "Weight on your Feet - 5 Times Heavier." Fjäderlätt. February 23, 2019. Accessed January 11, 2022. http://www.fjaderlatt.se/2009/11/weight-on-your-feet.html.

Jornet, Kilian. (2013). La Frontera Invisible. Barcelona: Ara Llibres SCCL.

Jornet, Kilian. (2013). Run or Die. Boulder: VeloPress.

Jornet, Kilian. (2018). Summits of My Life: Daring Adventures on the World's Greatest Peaks. Boulder: VeloPress.

Jurek, Scott, and Jenny Jurek. (2019). North: Finding My Way While Running the Appalachian Trail. Boston: Little, Brown and Company.

Jurek, Scott, and Steve Friedman. (2012). Eat and Run: My Unlikely Journey to Ultramarathon Greatness. Boston: Houghton Mifflin Harcourt.

Karnazes, Dean. (2006). Ultramarathon Man: Confessions of an All-Night Runner. London: Penguin Books Ltd.

Karnazes, Dean. (2009). 50/50: Secrets I Learned Running 50 Marathons in 50 Days—and How You Too Can Achieve Super Endurance. New York: Grand Central Publishing.

Karnazes, Dean. (2011). Run! 26.2 Stories of Blisters and Bliss. New York: Harmony/Rodale.

Karnazes, Dean. (2016). The Road to Sparta: Reliving the Ancient Battle and Epic Run That Inspired the World's Greatest Footrace. New York: Harmony/Rodale.

Macrotrends. (2022). "Canada Life Expectancy 1950-2022." Macrotrends. Accessed January 1, 2022. https://www.macrotrends.net/countries/CAN/canada/life-expectancy

Mayo Clinic. n.d. "Heat exhaustion." Mayo Clinic. Accessed January 12, 2022. https://www.mayoclinic.org/diseases-conditions/heat-exhaustion/symptoms-causes/syc-20373250.

McDougall, Christopher. (2011). Born to Run: A Hidden Tribe, Superathletes, and the Greatest Race the World Has Never Seen. New York City: Knopf Doubleday Publishing Group.

Miquel-Kergoat, Sophie, Veronique Azais-Braesco, Britt Burton-Freeman, and Marion M. Hetherington. (2015). "Effects of chewing on appetite, food intake and gut hormones: A systematic review and meta-analysis." Physiology & Behavior 1(151): 88–96. https://doi.org/10.1016/j.physbeh.2015.07.017

Mock, Justin. (2014). "Doubling the 100-Mile Distance." Runner's World. November 13, 2014. Accessed January 17, 2022. https://www.runnersworld.com/advanced/a20834977/doubling-the-100-mile-distance/.

Olson, Timothy. (2021). "PCT FKT Trail Report." Instagram. July 10, 2021. Accessed March 4, 2022. https://www.instagram.com/p/CRLBMS2Dtw3/

Partsch, Hugo, Johann Winiger, and Bertrand Lun. (2004). "Compression stockings reduce occupational leg swelling." Dermatologic Surgery 30(5): 737–743. https://doi.org/10.1111/j.1524-4725.2004.30204.x

Powell, Bryon. (2011). Relentless Forward Progress: A Guide to Running Ultramarathons. Halcottsville: Breakaway Books.

Preiato, Daniel. (2020). "Does Cortisol Affect Weight Gain?" Healthline. September 29, 2020. Accessed January 14, 2022. https://www.healthline.com/nutrition/cortisol-and-weight-gain.

Runner's World. (2018). "This is why Kipchoge smiles when he runs (and why you should be doing it too)." Runner's World. February 11, 2018. Accessed January 10, 2022. https://www.runnersworld.com/uk/training/motivation/a776539/how-smiling-improves-your-running/.

Sherrell, Zia. (2021). "What to know about fish oil benefits for bodybuilding." Medical News Today. March 9, 2021. Accessed 01 14, 2022. https://www.medicalnewstoday.com/articles/fish-oil-bodybuilding

Strout, Erin. (2015). "A Running Life: Ann Trason." Runner's World. May 25, 2015. Accessed January 17, 2022. https://www.runnersworld.com/advanced/a20789833/a-running-life-ann-trason/.

Superfeet. (2018). "Q and A with Ambassador Courtney Dauwalter: Pushing Limits, Searching for What's Possible." Superfeet. September 4, 2018. Accessed January 17, 2022. https://www.superfeet.com/en-us/blog/q-and-a-with-ultrarunner-courtney-dauwalter

Trail Runner (2017). "How Courtney Dauwalter Won the Moab 240 Outright." Trail Runner Magazine. October 19, 2017. Accessed April 14, 2022. https://www.trailrunnermag.com/people/news-people/courtney-dauwalter-wins-moab-240

Ulrich, Marshall. (2013). Running on Empty: An Ultramarathoner's Story of Love, Loss, and a Record-Setting Run Across America. New York: Putnam.

Ultrarunning Magazine. (2017). "Why We Won't Pay: UTMB, ITRA and the "Pay for Points" Racket." Ultrarunning Magazine. June 27, 2017. Accessed January 12, 2022. https://ultrarunning.com/ultrarunning-news/why-we-wont-pay-utmb-itra-and-the-pay-for-points-racket/.

Walters, Eric, and Ray Zahab. (2011). Just Deserts: One Teen. One Desert. One Epic Journey. Toronto: Penguin Random House Canada.

Yang, Billy. (2018). "Billy Yang Podcast." Rob Krar. [Podcast audio], August 18, 2018. https://billyyangpodcast.libsyn.com/rob-krar-byp-020

Zahab, Ray. n.d. 3 Beavers Racing. (website). Accessed January 14, 2022. https://www.3beaversracing.com/.

Zahab, Ray. (2007). Running for My Life: On the extreme road with adventure runner Ray Zahab. London, Ontario: Insomniac Press.

Zahab, Ray, and Steve Pitt. (2011). Running to Extremes: Ray Zahab's Amazing Ultramarathon Journey. Toronto, Ontario: PRH Canada Young Readers.

Acknowledgements

Writing this book felt like an ultramarathon in the huge amount of work that was required. Just like an ultramarathon, I could not have completed this book without the help from my support crew.

 A massive and heart felt thank you to my wife Lindsay for your unwavering support in all my crazy projects. Your encouragement and invaluable feedback were instrumental in bringing this book to life. You encourage me to move forward even when I have serious doubts. I am extremely grateful that you are my life partner.

 Thank you to my children, Norah, James, and David. You inspire me and help me keep perspective every day.

 To my parents Jann and Jim, thank you for believing in me without fail, for pushing me to do my best and for your endless compassion.

 Thank you to my sisters Jamie and Jacquie for always being amazing role models and supporters.

 Thank you to my editor and dear friend, Anne Marie Twiselton. You are a force of nature with your kindness, organization, professionalism, and attention to detail. You were instrumental in shaping this book and helping to make it something I am very proud of.

To Christopher Henderson, thank you for being an excellent friend and coach. I have benefitted greatly from your positive attitude, encouragement, and advice. I am very grateful for our random meeting on the trails, years ago.

To my in-laws, Sandra, and David, I appreciate all your assistance over the years. From looking after our children to watching my races, I am grateful for your support.

Thank you to my cover designer, Ellyl Faith Llavore. I am appreciative for your time and your high-quality work.

To Corinne Garlick and Peter Karas, thank you for designing the excellent Bruce Trail map. I am proud to have it in this book.

Finally, thank you to my team at work. Although some of my ultrarunning projects seem crazy, you have always had kind words to share with me.

Manufactured by Amazon.ca
Bolton, ON